The Indoor Grilling Cookbook

The Indoor Grilling Cookbook

100 Great Recipes for Electric and Stovetop Grills

General Editor Julie Stillman

Recipes Susan Herr, Lee Ann Cox, Susanne A. Davis

Photography Len Mastri

FOG CITY PRESS

Published by Fog City Press
814 Montgomery Street
San Francisco, CA 94133 USA

FOG CITY PRESS

Chief Executive Officer: John Owen
President: Terry Newell
Chief Operating Officer: Larry Partington
Associate Publisher: Hannah Rahill
Project Manager/Editor: Julie Stillman
Consulting Editor: Norman Kolpas
Business Manager: Emily Jahn
Vice President International Sales: Stuart Laurence
Copy Editor: Debra Hudak
Design: Faith Hague
Production: Chris Hemesath
Proofreader: Maggie Carr
Indexer: Michael Loo
Photography: Len Mastri
Food & Prop Stylist: Melissa McClelland
Introduction by: Susan Herr
Cover Design by: Sarah Gifford
Front Cover Photograph by: Daniel Clark
Front Cover Food Stylist: Pouké
Additional credits on page 260

A Weldon Owen Production

10 9 8 7 6 5 4 3 2 1

Library of Congress Cataloging-in-Publication Data is available.

ISBN 1-892374-53-6

Printed in Singapore by Kyodo Printing Co. (S'pore) Pte Ltd

Contributors

General Editor

Julie Stillman is a Vermont-based freelance editor and book packager with over twenty years' experience in book publishing. She is the author of *A Celebration of Women Chefs* (Ten Speed Press).

Recipe Developers

Susan Herr is a recipe developer, editor, and food stylist. She is the former Test Kitchen Manager at *Eating Well* magazine and has worked as an editor for Tavolo.com and *Woman's Day* Special Interest Publications.

Lee Ann Cox is former Senior Editor of *Eating Well* magazine and Executive Editor of Tavolo.com. Her work has appeared in *The New York Times*, *Food Arts*, and *Weight Watchers* magazine.

Susanne A. Davis, a graduate of the New England Culinary Institute, is a freelance recipe developer and food stylist. She is the former Test Kitchen Manager at *Eating Well* magazine.

Photographer

Len Mastri is a commercial photographer specializing in food photography. His clients include Ben & Jerry's, King Arthur Flour, and Hachette-Fillipachi publications. He is the photographer for *A Celebration of Women Chefs*.

Contents

Introduction to Indoor Grilling

A s a cooking technique, indoor grilling is hard to beat. It's fast, it's flavorful, it's healthful, and unlike the outdoor version, it's not dependent on the weather or season.

You can make the basics like crisp-crusted grilled cheese sandwiches or juicy burgers in just minutes, without any added fat. Zap up the flavor of favorite dishes by grilling some of the ingredients, like tomatoes for a simple salsa. Or create a whole meal by grilling several courses side by side or in succession.

This cookbook is full of fabulous recipes developed especially for indoor grilling—from simple steaks and kabobs to grilled fish and vegetarian entrees, to grilled fruit desserts. There are lots of quick and easy recipes for weeknight family suppers, plus others exotic enough for stress-free weekend entertaining. Many of the recipes call for marinades or sauces that can be made in advance, so all you need to do is preheat the grill and you're ready to go. A chapter featuring side dishes and accompaniments (not grilled) makes *The Indoor Grilling Cookbook* your one-stop source for complete meals.

Here's some basic know-how to get you on your way.

Equipment

The popularity of grilling indoors and out has soared, and so has the range of grilling tools. While the choice of machines, pans, and range-top units for indoor grilling may seem confusing, there are only two basic types: those that grill on one side at a time and those that grill on both sides at once.

Grill pans, one-sided electric indoor grills, and vented gas or electric grills which are part of a stovetop all cook the food with intense heat on one side at a time. Two-sided electric grills cook the food simultaneously from the top and bottom, cutting the cooking time in half.

When choosing a piece of equipment, keep in mind that grill pans can be easier to store, but the smoke they produce requires a good exhaust system. Electric grills have a receptacle to catch any fat and juices that drip away, which makes them almost smoke-free.

Using and Caring for an Electric Indoor Grill

Be sure to read the instructions that come with your particular machine. To protect the nonstick cooking surface, always use nylon or wooden utensils to maneuver foods, or use metal tongs but be careful not to scratch the grill plates. Place the grill on a dry and level surface, with its cord safely out of the way, and always unplug it when it is not in use.

Some machines have removable grill plates that can go in the sink or dishwasher for cleaning. If the plates are not removable, let the machine cool after cooking, then place it next to the sink and swab the cooking surfaces with hot soapy water. Let it stand for a few minutes so the baked-on particles soften, then wipe it clean with a wet sponge or cloth. Repeat with more hot soapy water as necessary.

Using and Caring for a Grill Pan

Grill pans have a ridged surface, which allows the food to sit up off the bottom of the pan as the fat collects below. They come in square, rectangular, and round shapes, and can be made of cast iron, metal, or enameled metal, often with a nonstick surface. A large grill pan is more versatile because it can accommodate more food.

Cast-iron pans without a nonstick surface should be "seasoned" before using, to keep them from rusting and to prevent foods from sticking. To season a new cast-iron pan, scrub it in hot soapy water with a nylon or plastic brush or scrubber, then dry it completely. Rub it inside and out with solid vegetable shortening. Put the pan in a 300°F (150°C) oven to bake for 15 minutes; remove the pan from the oven and carefully pour off any excess melted shortening. Return it to the oven and bake for one hour longer. Let the pan cool slowly in the turned-off oven. After each use, clean the pan with hot soapy water, scrubbing if necessary; never put it in the dishwasher. Dry it with a towel and store it in a dry place to avoid rust. You may want to brush the pan lightly with oil the first few times you use it; as it ages, it will develop a darker color and become increasingly "nonstick." Most other grill pans have a nonstick coating and require no seasoning.

Tips for Great Grilling

✦ Both the electric indoor grill and the grill pan should be preheated for several minutes or according to the manufacturer's instructions before the food is added; this ensures that the outside of the food will sear quickly, forming a flavorful surface.

✦ Even if the machine or pan has a nonstick surface, a light brush of oil or spritz of nonstick cooking spray may be needed to prevent lean foods from sticking or to give them better color. Oil or spray the grill or pan before heating, or oil or spray foods just before cooking; never spray directly onto a hot grill or pan. A coating of fresh or dry breadcrumbs on foods can also add color and prevent sticking.

✦ For even cooking on the two-sided grill, food should be of an even thickness. Choose salmon steaks of the same thickness, for instance, or flatten uneven meats like boneless chicken breasts into a thinner and more even layer by placing them between two pieces of plastic wrap and pounding them with a heavy pan or rolling pin. Small poultry such as chicken or game hens should be cut in half lengthwise and firmly pressed into a more even layer.

If you have a layer of food, such as sliced potatoes, distribute it evenly over the surface of the pan or grill and turn and rearrange it about halfway through the cooking time so the heat reaches all of the slices evenly.

✦ Avoid foods that are too thick, because the heat may take too long to reach the center. A small boneless turkey breast half, for instance, is fine for a two-sided grill, where the heat is penetrating from both sides, but not for an open grill pan.

✦ Sweet marinades, sauces, or glazes will burn on the grill before the food is cooked, so avoid them altogether or brush them on toward the end of the cooking time.

✦ Bamboo skewers are great for kabobs. If you are using the grill pan or other one-sided equipment, the skewers should be presoaked in water for at least 30 minutes to prevent them from scorching. Because of the shorter cooking time on the two-sided grill, it's not necessary to soak the skewers. (See page 19 for more information on skewers.)

✦ Cut foods for kabobs into uniform sizes and shapes. Use tender vegetables such as mushrooms or cherry tomatoes on kabobs that will cook as quickly as the meat or fish you are combining them with. Or thread each item on a separate skewer, removing each skewer as it is done. When threading the skewers, leave a little space between each item to allow uniform heat penetration.

Cooking Times for Indoor Grilling

The following times are offered as guidelines only. Times will vary with individual electric grills, pans, and stoves.

Item	Two-Sided Electric Grill	Grill Pan
Chicken breast half, boneless and skinless, 4 ounces (125 g)	4 to 5 minutes	8 to 10 minutes
Chicken breast half, bone-in	6 to 8 minutes	12 to 15 minutes
Chicken thighs, boneless	4 to 5 minutes	8 to 10 minutes
Chicken thighs, bone-in	8 to 10 minutes	15 to 20 minutes
Cut-up whole chicken	15 to 18 minutes	20 to 25 minutes
Chicken kabobs	2 to 3 minutes	4 to 6 minutes
Turkey breast cutlets	4 minutes	8 to 10 minutes
Duck breast, boneless, 6 ounces (185 g)	4 to 6 minutes	8 to 12 minutes
Ground beef or poultry patties, 4 ounces (125 g)	4 to 7 minutes	8 to 14 minutes
Beef steak, boneless, 1 inch (2.5 cm) thick	4 to 5 minutes for medium rare	8 to 10 minutes for medium rare
London broil, 1¼ inches (3 cm) thick	8 minutes for medium rare	18 to 20 minutes for medium rare
Beef or lamb kabobs	2 to 3 minutes for medium rare	4 to 6 minutes for medium rare

Item	Two-Sided Electric Grill	Grill Pan
Lamb chops, rib or loin, 1 inch (2.5 cm) thick	6 to 8 minutes for medium rare	10 to 14 minutes for medium rare
Whole pork tenderloin, 12 ounces (375 g)	8 minutes	15 minutes
Country-style pork spareribs, bone-in	10 to 12 minutes	18 to 20 minutes
Pork chops, rib or loin, ¾ to 1 inch (2 to 2.5 cm) thick	6 to 8 minutes	12 to 15 minutes
Pork chops, ½ inch (12 mm) thick	3 to 4 minutes	6 minutes
Hot dogs	2½ to 3 minutes	5 to 6 minutes
Sea scallops	2½ to 4 minutes	5 to 8 minutes
Shrimp, large	2 to 3 minutes	5 to 8 minutes
Fish fillets or steaks	2 to 3 minutes per ½ inch of thickness	4 to 6 minutes per ½ inch of thickness
Grilled cheese sandwich	2 minutes	4 to 5 minutes
Potato slices, ¼ inch (6 mm) thick	12 to 15 minutes	15 to 20 minutes, covered with foil
Bell peppers, sliced	4 to 5 minutes	8 to 10 minutes
Mushrooms, button	2 to 3 minutes	6 to 8 minutes
Mushrooms, portobello	3 to 4 minutes	6 to 8 minutes

How to Tell When Foods Are Done

Cooking times given in recipes are only guidelines, and variables like the material and thickness of a pan or the wattage of a particular grill will greatly affect how quickly the food cooks. It is important to check foods often; overcooked foods can become dry or tough, especially delicate foods like fish or lean foods like pork tenderloin. Undercooked foods, especially ground meats or pork products, can harbor dangerous microorganisms. Remember, foods continue to cook for a while after they are removed from the heat, so you can take them from the grill just before the desired degree of doneness has been reached.

✦ Poultry should be opaque throughout, with no traces of pink in the flesh or juices. To check, make a small cut into the thickest part. For larger pieces, insert an instant-read thermometer into the thickest part (not touching bone); breast meat should be at least 170°F (77°C), and dark meat should be at least 180°F (82°C). Ground chicken or turkey patties should reach 165°F (74°C) in the center.

✦ For beef, veal, and lamb, make an incision into the thickest part to see if it has reached the desired degree of doneness. If using an instant-read thermometer, the United States Department of Agriculture (USDA) recommends these meats should register 145°F (63°C) for medium rare, 160°F (71°C) for medium, and 170°F (77°C) for well done. Ground beef patties should register 160°F (71°C) in the center.

- Pork should register 160°F (71°C) on the thermometer for medium and 170°F (77°C) for well done. For moist, tender results, a slight trace of rosiness should remain in the center.

- Fish should not be overcooked or it will lose its delicate flavor and texture. Insert a fork or the tip of a sharp knife at the thickest part to see if the fish is just losing its translucency and is just pulling apart into flakes.

- Vegetables and potatoes are generally done when they can be easily pierced with a toothpick or skewer. This is especially important for eggplant, which has an unpleasant astringent quality when undercooked.

Food Safety

- While some cookbooks suggest marinating foods at room temperature or removing them from the refrigerator to warm to room temperature before grilling, this is not recommended by the USDA; bacterial growth can occur when food is above 40°F (4°C).

- Poultry can be marinated in the refrigerator, well-covered, for one to two days. Red meat can be marinated for three to five days. Marinating in food-safe resealable plastic bags makes cleanup easy, but be sure to discard the bags after use.

- If a marinade is to be used subsequently for basting or as a sauce, boil it for a few minutes to destroy any bacteria from the raw ingredients. Never reuse a marinade for a new batch of raw food.

- Don't put cooked foods back on a cutting board or platter that has just held raw foods.
- Wash your hands before and after handling raw meat, poultry, fish, and eggs.
- Remember that ground meats are particularly susceptible to bacterial contamination because of all the surfaces exposed during the grinding process. Always cook ground meats thoroughly—until there is no trace of pink in the center.
- When entertaining, don't leave cooked foods out at room temperature for more than two hours.

How to Use This Book

Most of the recipes in this book will work with either a two-sided electric grill or a single-sided heat source such as a grill pan. Each recipe indicates the appropriate equipment: for the two-sided grill, for the grill pan. Those recipes appropriate for the grill pan can also be made using other single-sided equipment, though you should check the cooking times recommended by the manufacturer of your particular grill.

The recipes were designed to yield four servings, so the larger-size grills and grill pans are recommended. A few recipes specifically call for a large grill or grill pan, such as Chicken Cacciatore on the Grill (page 70), because meat and vegetables are being cooked at the same time. If you have a smaller-size grill, you could cook the food in batches. If you are cooking for two or one, you'll find that most recipes can easily be cut in half.

You'll find quite a few recipes for kabobs in these pages. Because of the many different types, sizes, and shapes of indoor grilling equipment, we do not give specific information as to the length or type (wooden, bamboo, or metal) of skewer to use. Generally you would use the longer 12-inch skewers for larger-size grills and 6-inch skewers for smaller grills. It is recommended that you *not* use metal skewers in the two-sided grill, because these bulkier skewers may keep the grill from closing completely.

All recipes include customary U.S, U.K., and metric measurements. Metric conversions are based on a standard developed by the publisher and have been rounded off. Actual weights may vary.

Suggested Menus

Simple Suppers

Barbecued Country-Style Ribs (page 124)
Coleslaw
Baked Beans
Corn Bread (page 237)

~

Grilled Rosemary-Citrus Chicken (page 42)
Saffron Rice (page 231)
Butternut Squash Puree
Sesame-Green Bean Salad (page 230)

~

Sesame Salmon Steaks (page 192)
Spicy Peanut Noodles (page 236)
Asian Slaw (page 226)

~

Grilled Steak in Red Wine Marinade (page 94)
Sautéed Zucchini
Old-Fashioned Potato Salad (page 234)

Easy Entertaining

Beef Tenderloin Steaks with Horseradish Sauce (112)
Garlic Mashed Potatoes
Tomato, Mozzarella & Basil Salad (page 227)
Grilled Pears with Balsamic Vinegar & Goat Cheese (page 244)

∼

Pork Tenderloin with Pineapple-Chipotle Glaze (page 156)
Roasted Sweet Potatoes
Black Beans & Rice
Salad of Mixed Greens
Grilled Peach Melba (page 248)

∼

Bruschetta with Tomatoes, Beans, & Fresh Herbs (page 238)
Shrimp Skewers with Mango Salsa (page 174)
Basmati Rice
Spinach & Avocado Salad
Butter-Rum Grilled Bananas (page 250)

∼

Mexican Beer or Margaritas
Black Bean Quesadillas (page 218)
Margarita Steak with Grilled Onion Guacamole (page 110)
Jicama-Orange Salad
Grilled Pineapple Sundae (page 242)

Sauces, Rubs, and Marinades

Texas Barbecue Sauce

Serve this classic sauce on grilled chicken, brisket, or hamburgers, either as a baste or a table sauce.

MAKES ABOUT
1½ CUPS
(12 fl oz/375 ml)

2 teaspoons vegetable oil

1 small onion, finely diced

1 cup (8 oz/250 g) ketchup

½ cup (4 fl oz/125 ml) brewed coffee

2 tablespoons molasses

2 tablespoons cider vinegar

2 tablespoons Worcestershire sauce

2 teaspoons Dijon mustard

½ teaspoon hot pepper sauce

✦ In a small saucepan, heat the oil over medium heat. Add the onion and sauté until softened, about 5 minutes. Add remaining ingredients and stir well. Simmer over low heat for 30 minutes. Let cool. The sauce will keep, covered, in the refrigerator for up to 1 week.

photograph on page 50

Quick Tomato Salsa

You won't find a salsa recipe that's easier to make than this one!

MAKES ABOUT
1¼ CUPS
(10 fl oz/310 ml)

4 ripe Italian plum tomatoes, seeded and coarsely
    chopped
2 fresh serrano chiles, stemmed and coarsely chopped
¼ cup (2 fl oz/60 ml) fresh lime juice
1 teaspoon salt
½ teaspoon freshly ground black pepper

◆ In a food processor, combine all the ingredients.
   Process to the desired texture.

Romesco Sauce

A rich, robust sauce from the Catalonia region of Spain that is excellent served on grilled vegetables, fish, chicken, or lamb.

MAKES 2 CUPS
(16 fl oz/500 ml)

2 large cloves garlic, unpeeled
2 large dried New Mexican or Ancho chiles
1 slice country-style bread, 1 inch (2.5 cm) thick
$1/4$ cup (2 fl oz/60 ml) plus 1 tablespoon olive oil
1 red bell pepper
2 ripe tomatoes, cored and quartered lengthwise
$1/3$ cup (2 oz/57 g) almonds, toasted
2 tablespoons sherry vinegar or red wine vinegar
1 teaspoon salt
Freshly ground black pepper
Pinch of cayenne pepper
2 tablespoons finely chopped fresh parsley

✦ Heat a grill pan or sauté pan over medium-high heat. Place the garlic to one side of the pan and grill, turning occasionally, until softened, about 20 minutes. When cool, peel the garlic.

✦ Meanwhile, stem the chiles. Make a cut down one side, open them out flat, and shake out the seeds. Bring a small saucepan of water to a boil. Place the chiles in the grill pan, press them flat with a metal spatula, and grill them until they are toasted, 2 to 3 minutes, turning once. Add the chiles to the boiling water, turn off the heat, and set the saucepan aside for 30 minutes.

✦ Brush the bread on both sides with 1 teaspoon of the oil. Grill until it is lightly toasted on both sides. Set aside. Cook the red bell pepper, in the pan or directly over a gas flame, until it is well charred on all sides. When it is cool enough to handle, peel, stem, and seed it.

✦ Brush the tomato quarters on all sides with 2 teaspoons of the oil. Place them in the grill pan and cook, turning frequently, until they are very soft and blackened in spots, about 10 minutes.

✦ Tear the bread into pieces and place in a food processor with the peeled garlic and the almonds. Process until finely ground. Drain the chiles and add them to the processor with the tomatoes, roasted pepper, vinegar, salt, black pepper to taste, and cayenne pepper. Process the mixture until smooth. With the machine running, pour the remaining 1/4 cup (2 fl oz/60 ml) of oil through the feed tube. Stir in the parsley. Transfer the sauce to an airtight container. It will keep in the refrigerator for up to 3 days.

Smooth Red Salsa

This is not the usual chunky tomato salsa, but a smoother, more sophisticated sauce. It may be served warm or at room temperature, as a table salsa or as a topping for simple grilled chicken or fish.

MAKES ABOUT
1½ CUPS
(12 fl oz/375 ml)

2 tablespoons vegetable oil
1 small yellow onion, thinly sliced
2 cloves garlic, thinly sliced
1 jalapeño chile, stemmed, seeded, and thinly sliced
1 teaspoon salt
1½ cups (12 fl oz/375 g) canned plum tomatoes, with juice

✦ In a saucepan, heat the oil over medium heat. Add the onion and cook, stirring occasionally, until softened, about 10 minutes. Add the garlic, jalapeño, and salt and cook for 2 minutes more.

✦ Add the tomatoes with their juice, reduce the heat to low and continue cooking, stirring occasionally, until the tomatoes are soft and the liquid has reduced by half.

✦ Let the mixture cool slightly, then transfer it to a blender and puree until smooth.

✦ Set a strainer over a bowl and pour the mixture through. Serve warm or at room temperature. Store tightly covered in the refrigerator for up to 4 days or in the freezer for up to 1 month.

sauces, rubs & marinades

Mexican Spice Paste

Ground nuts and toasted sesame seeds often enrich Mexican dishes, and peanut butter and sesame oil are handy sources for those flavors. Brush this paste generously over boneless chicken breasts, medallions of pork tenderloin, or slices of turkey breast before grilling. Serve with wedges of fresh lime for squeezing over the top.

Makes about ½ cup
(4 fl oz/125 g)

2 tablespoons mild pure chili powder
1 tablespoon hot pure chili powder
1 teaspoon salt
1 teaspoon ground cumin
$1/2$ teaspoon ground cinnamon
$1/2$ teaspoon ground coriander
$1/8$ teaspoon ground cloves
3 tablespoons olive or vegetable oil
2 tablespoons peanut butter
1 tablespoon fresh lime juice
2 teaspoons dark sesame oil

✦ In a small bowl, whisk together the chili powders, salt, cumin, cinnamon, coriander, and cloves.

✦ Add the oil, peanut butter, lime juice, and sesame oil and whisk until smooth. Store tightly covered in the refrigerator for up to 1 week.

photograph on page 50

Vindaloo Paste

*This hot blend of
Indian spices works
well with meat.*

MAKES ABOUT ½ CUP
(4 fl oz/125 g)

¹/₄ cup (2 fl oz/60 ml) white vinegar

2 teaspoons ground cumin

2 teaspoons turmeric

2 teaspoons hot mustard, smooth or coarse-grain

1 teaspoon ground cardamom

1 teaspoon seeded and minced red or green chile

1 teaspoon ground cinnamon

✦ In a small bowl, stir all the ingredients together until smooth. Brush evenly over meat before grilling.

Middle Eastern Spice Rub

*An exotic blend of
familiar spices is
perfect on chicken
or lamb kabobs.*

MAKES ABOUT ½ CUP
(4 fl oz/125 g)

2 tablespoons ground cumin

4 teaspoons freshly ground black pepper

4 teaspoons ground turmeric

2 teaspoons ground cinnamon

2 teaspoons coarse salt

✦ In a small dish, combine all the ingredients. Store in an airtight container at room temperature.

photograph on page 50

North African Spice Paste

Brush this spicy blend generously over chicken, fish, or lamb before grilling. Chopped fresh cilantro makes a delicious garnish.

MAKES ABOUT
3 TABLESPOONS

2 teaspoons minced garlic
2 teaspoons minced fresh ginger
$1/2$ teaspoon salt
2 tablespoons olive oil
1 tablespoon mild paprika
1 teaspoon ground cumin
$1/4$ teaspoon cayenne pepper

✦ Using a mortar and pestle, combine the garlic, ginger, and salt; mash to a paste. (Alternatively, use a chef's knife and a combination of chopping and mashing with the flat side of the knife to make the paste.)

✦ Transfer the paste to a small bowl and add the oil, paprika, cumin, and cayenne pepper; stir together thoroughly.

✦ Refrigerate in a tightly covered container for up to 1 week.

To make any of the following marinades, simply mix all the ingredients together thoroughly. Place the item to be marinated in a glass or other nonreactive dish or resealable plastic bag, add the marinade and turn the food to coat it well. (Do not use a metal dish—acids will react with the metal, producing an unpleasant taste.) Store the dish, covered, in the refrigerator for 2 to 12 hours. Shake off the excess marinade before cooking. The remaining marinade can be used for basting the meat as it is cooking, but you need to boil the marinade for several minutes to destroy any bacteria. Each of these recipes makes a quantity sufficient to marinate 4 servings of meat.

Mediterranean Marinade

MAKES ABOUT
1¼ CUPS
(10 fl oz/310 ml)

3 cloves garlic, minced

½ cup (4 oz/125 g) tomato paste

½ cup (4 fl oz/125 ml) olive oil

¼ cup (2 fl oz/60 ml) red wine

2 teaspoons dried oregano

Horseradish Marinade

MAKES ABOUT $^1/_3$ CUP
(3 fl oz/80 ml)

$^1/_2$ cup (4 fl oz/125 ml) white wine

1 tablespoon canola oil

1 tablespoon horseradish

2 teaspoons chopped fresh cilantro leaves

2 teaspoons coarse-grain mustard

Citrus Marinade

MAKES ABOUT
$1^1/_3$ CUPS
(11 fl oz/330 ml)

$^2/_3$ cup (5 fl oz/160 ml) grapefruit juice

$^1/_3$ cup (3 fl oz/80 ml) orange juice

$^1/_3$ cup (3 fl oz/80 ml) olive oil

A few drops of sesame oil (optional)

1 teaspoon minced garlic

1 teaspoon hot paprika

1 tablespoon brown sugar or honey

Honey-Mint Marinade

MAKES ABOUT 1/3 CUP
(3 fl oz/80 ml)

2 tablespoons fresh lemon juice

2 tablespoons chopped fresh mint leaves

4 teaspoons honey

1–2 teaspoons seeded and minced red or green chile pepper

1 teaspoon sesame oil

Five-Spice Marinade

MAKES ABOUT I CUP
(8 fl oz/250 ml)

1/4 cup (2 fl/60 ml) honey

1/4 cup dry sherry

1/4 cup soy sauce

2 teaspoons sesame oil

2 teaspoons Chinese five-spice powder

2 teaspoons minced garlic

2 teaspoons minced ginger

Garlic-Oregano Marinade

MAKES ABOUT ½ CUP
(4 fl oz/125 g)

2 tablespoons olive oil

2 tablespoons dry Italian white wine

4–6 teaspoons fresh oregano leaves or 2–3 teaspoons
    dried

6 large cloves garlic, minced

Red pepper flakes or cayenne pepper

photograph on page 50

Red Wine Marinade

MAKES ABOUT 3 CUPS
(24 fl oz/750 ml)

1¼ cups (10 fl oz/310 ml) dry red wine

1 cup (8 fl oz/250 ml) olive oil

¼ cup (2 fl oz/60 ml) port wine

2 tablespoons balsamic vinegar

2 tablespoons Dijon mustard

1 large clove garlic, minced

1 onion, sliced

1 bay leaf, crumbled

A few sprigs parsley

1 tablespoon brown sugar

½ teaspoon black peppercorns

Poultry

Grilled Sesame Chicken

*When served with
Spicy Peanut
Noodles (page 236),
green beans
sautéed with ginger
and garlic, and an
Asian cucumber
salad, these chicken
breasts make for
easy entertaining
or a nice supper on
a hot summer
evening.*

<small>SERVES 4</small>

For the marinade

2 tablespoons toasted sesame oil

1 tablespoon Chinese rice wine or dry sherry

1 tablespoon rice wine vinegar

1 teaspoon soy sauce

1 teaspoon minced garlic

1 teaspoon minced fresh ginger

For the chicken

4 boneless, skinless chicken breast halves,
about $1^1/_4$ pounds (625 g)

2 teaspoons sesame seeds

◆ To make the marinade, in a small bowl whisk together all the marinade ingredients.

◆ Place the chicken breasts in a resealable plastic bag and add the marinade. Seal the bag and marinate for 1 to 8 hours in the refrigerator, turning occasionally.

◆ In a 350°F (180°C) oven or in a skillet over medium-high heat, toast the sesame seeds until golden and fragrant, 2 to 3 minutes. Transfer to a small plate to cool.

◆ Preheat a two-sided electric indoor grill or ridged grill pan according to the manufacturer's instructions.

◆ Remove the chicken from the marinade, shaking off the excess.

◆ **If you are using the two-sided grill,** place the chicken on the grill, close the cover, and cook until the chicken is browned and opaque in the center, 4 to 5 minutes.

◆ **If you are using the grill pan,** cook the chicken until it is browned and opaque in the center, 8 to 10 minutes, turning it once midway through the cooking time.

◆ Sprinkle the chicken with sesame seeds and serve, or for a prettier presentation, cut the chicken breasts into thin slices.

Firecracker Chicken Thighs

Hot bean paste adds heat and richness to the marinade; look for it in the Asian section of the grocery store or at an Asian market. Serve the chicken with snow peas and an aromatic rice such as jasmine or basmati.

For the marinade

2 tablespoons sesame seeds
$^1/_4$ cup ($1^1/_4$ oz/40 g) finely chopped scallions
4 large cloves garlic, finely chopped
2–3 tablespoons hot bean paste or sauce
2 tablespoons soy sauce
1 tablespoon sesame oil
1 tablespoon sugar
$^1/_8$ teaspoon freshly ground black pepper

For the chicken

6 bone-in chicken thighs

+ In a 350°F (180°C) oven or in a skillet over medium-high heat, toast the sesame seeds until golden and fragrant, 2 to 3 minutes. Transfer to a small plate to cool.

+ To make the marinade, using a mortar and pestle crush the sesame seeds. Transfer them to a bowl and add the scallions, garlic, bean paste or sauce, soy sauce, sesame oil, sugar, and pepper; stir them together well.

+ To prepare the chicken, pull off and discard the skin from the chicken thighs. With a sharp paring knife, cut off any excess fat and score the meat on both sides with shallow diagonal cuts about 1 inch (2.5 cm) apart. Add the chicken to the marinade and turn to coat it. Cover and refrigerate for 4 to 24 hours, turning the chicken occasionally.

+ Preheat a two-sided electric indoor grill or ridged grill pan according to the manufacturer's instructions.

+ Remove the chicken from the marinade, shaking off the excess.

+ **If you are using the two-sided grill,** place the chicken on the grill, close the cover, and cook, in batches as necessary, until the chicken is no longer pink in the center, 8 to 10 minutes.

+ **If you are using the grill pan,** cook, in batches as necessary, until the chicken is no longer pink in the center, 15 to 20 minutes, turning it once midway through the cooking time.

Grilled Rosemary-Citrus Chicken

*For a delicious,
elegant dinner,
serve the chicken
over a bed of
wild rice
accompanied by
quickly sautéed
zucchini ribbons in
the summer or
butternut squash
puree in winter.*

SERVES 4

For the marinade

$1/3$ cup (3 fl oz/80 ml) olive oil

$1/3$ cup (3 fl oz/80 ml) orange juice

$1/4$ cup (2 fl oz/60 ml) fresh lemon juice

1 tablespoon chopped fresh rosemary or
   $1^{1}/2$ teaspoons dried rosemary, crushed

2 cloves garlic, minced

$1/2$ teaspoon salt

$1/4$ teaspoon freshly ground black pepper

For the chicken

4 boneless, skinless chicken breast halves,
   about 1 pound (500 g) total

4 large sprigs fresh rosemary for garnish (optional)

◆ To make the marinade, in a small bowl, combine the olive oil, orange juice, lemon juice, rosemary, garlic, salt, and pepper and whisk well. Pour into a shallow, nonreactive dish, add the chicken breasts and turn to coat. Cover and refrigerate for 2 to 6 hours.

◆ Preheat a two-sided electric indoor grill or ridged grill pan according to the manufacturer's instructions.

◆ Remove the chicken from the marinade, shaking off the excess.

◆ **If you are using the two-sided grill,** place the chicken on the grill, close the cover, and cook until the chicken is no longer pink in the center, about 4 minutes.

◆ **If you are using the grill pan**, cook the chicken until it is no longer pink in the center, 8 to 10 minutes, turning it once midway through the cooking time.

◆ Serve immediately, garnished with rosemary sprigs, if desired.

Spicy Chicken Kabobs

A great dish for a busy weeknight, this recipe is fast and flavorful. Saffron Rice (page 231) is the perfect accompaniment.

SERVES 4

For the marinade

¹/₄ cup (2 fl oz/60 ml) canola oil

3 tablespoons fresh lemon juice

2 tablespoons chopped fresh parsley

¹/₂ teaspoon paprika

¹/₂ teaspoon ground cumin

¹/₂ teaspoon salt

¹/₄ teaspoon freshly ground black pepper

¹/₄ teaspoon cayenne pepper

Pinch of saffron threads, crumbled (optional)

For the kabobs

8 boneless, skinless chicken thighs, trimmed of fat and cut into 1-inch (2.5-cm) cubes

Lemon wedges for garnish

photograph on page 51

◆ To make the marinade, in a medium bowl whisk together the oil, lemon juice, parsley, paprika, cumin, salt, black pepper, cayenne pepper, and saffron (if using). Add the chicken and stir to coat. Cover with plastic wrap and marinate in the refrigerator, turning occasionally for 4 to 24 hours.

◆ Preheat a two-sided electric indoor grill or ridged grill pan according to the manufacturer's instructions.

◆ **If you are using the two-sided grill,** thread the marinated chicken onto skewers, leaving a little space between the pieces. Place the skewers on the grill, close the cover, and cook, in batches as necessary, until the chicken is no longer pink in the center, about 4 minutes.

◆ **If you are using the grill pan,** thread the marinated chicken onto skewers, leaving a little space between the pieces. Cook in batches as necessary, until the chicken is no longer pink in the center, about 6 minutes, turning it once midway through the cooking time.

◆ Serve with lemon wedges.

Chipotle-Orange Chicken Breasts

*Rice and beans
and some sliced
avocado would be
perfect with this
lively Southwestern
dish.*

SERVES 4

For the marinade

$^1/_2$ cup (4 fl oz/125 ml) orange juice

1 tablespoon fresh lime juice

$^1/_2$ dried chipotle chile, stemmed and seeded

$^1/_2$ cup (4 fl oz/125 ml) Smooth Red Salsa (page 28)

2 tablespoons olive oil

1 teaspoon salt

For the chicken

4 boneless, skinless chicken breast halves,
about 1 pound (500 g) total

Fresh orange slices and cilantro sprigs, for garnish
(optional)

photograph on page 49

✦ To make the marinade, in a small saucepan combine the orange juice, lime juice, and chile and bring the mixture to a boil; reduce the heat to maintain a simmer and cook, uncovered, until the chile is softened, about 5 minutes. Remove from the heat and let cool completely.

✦ Transfer the mixture to a blender and add the salsa, oil, and salt. Blend until smooth and the liquid has reduced by half, 10 to 15 minutes.

✦ To prepare the chicken, place the chicken breasts between two sheets of plastic wrap; pound them with a heavy pan or rolling pin to flatten. Place the chicken in a shallow, nonreactive dish and add the marinade, turning the chicken to coat it. Cover and refrigerate for 2 to 4 hours.

✦ Preheat a two-sided electric indoor grill or ridged grill pan according to the manufacturer's instructions.

✦ Remove the chicken from the marinade, shaking off the excess.

✦ **If you are using the two-sided grill,** place the chicken on the grill, close the cover, and cook until the chicken is no longer pink in the center, 4 to 5 minutes.

✦ **If you are using the grill pan,** cook the chicken until it is no longer pink in the center, 8 to 10 minutes, turning it once midway through the cooking time.

✦ Transfer the chicken to a platter and garnish with orange slices and cilantro, if desired.

Chipotle-Orange Chicken Breasts
Page 46

Garlic-Oregano Marinade,
Middle Eastern Spice Rub,
Horseradish Marinade, Mexican Spice
Paste, Texas Barbecue Sauce
Pages 35, 30, 33, 29, 24

Spicy Chicken Kabobs
Page 44

**Grilled Chicken Breasts
with Walnut-Sage Pesto**
Page 64

Chicken Cacciatore on the Grill
Page 70

**Grilled Duck Breasts
with Cranberry-Pear Compote**
Page 86

**Turkey Breast
with Spinach-Couscous
Stuffing**
Page 84

Grilled Chicken & Bread Salad
Opposite

Grilled Chicken & Bread Salad

All the elements of this hearty main-course salad can be prepared a few hours ahead. Just be sure to have the vinaigrette and the grilled chicken at room temperature and toss everything together at the last minute.

SERVES 4

photo opposite

For the vinaigrette

1/4 cup (2 fl oz/60 ml) fresh lemon juice

1 teaspoon Dijon mustard

1 clove garlic, minced

6 tablespoons (3 fl oz/90 ml) extra-virgin olive oil

1 teaspoon salt, plus more as needed

Freshly ground black pepper

1/3 cup (2 oz/60 g) golden raisins

For the salad

3 tablespoons olive oil, divided

1 pound (500 g) boneless, skinless chicken breasts

Salt and freshly ground black pepper

3 slices best-quality country-style white or sourdough bread, 1 inch (2.5 cm) thick

4 cups (3/4 lb/375 g) hearty salad greens (such as frisée), stemmed and torn into pieces

1/2 cup (2 oz/60 g) walnuts, toasted and chopped

1/4 cup (3/8 oz/10 g) chopped fresh parsley

continued on page 58

+ To make the vinaigrette, in a medium bowl whisk the lemon juice, mustard, and garlic together. Whisking constantly, slowly drizzle in the olive oil. Whisk in 1 teaspoon salt, and pepper to taste. Reserve $1/4$ cup (2 fl oz/60 ml) of the vinaigrette. Add the raisins to the remaining vinaigrette in the bowl and set aside.

+ Preheat a two-sided electric indoor grill or ridged grill pan according to the manufacturer's instructions.

+ Rub 1 tablespoon of the olive oil over both sides of the chicken and season with salt and pepper.

+ **If you are using the two-sided grill,** place the chicken on the grill, close the cover, and cook until the chicken is no longer pink in the center, 4 to 5 minutes. Set aside to cool.

+ **If you are using the grill pan,** cook until the chicken is no longer pink in the center, 8 to 10 minutes, turning it once midway through the cooking time. Set aside to cool.

+ Meanwhile, brush the remaining 2 tablespoons olive oil over both sides of the bread slices. Grill the bread until nicely browned, about 2 minutes per side in the grill pan or 1 minute on the two-sided grill. Cut into 1-inch (2.5-cm) cubes.

+ To assemble the salad, toss the salad greens with the reserved $1/4$ cup (2 fl oz/60 ml) vinaigrette. Cut the chicken on the diagonal into $1/2$-inch (12-mm)-thick slices. Toss the chicken, bread, walnuts, and parsley with the raisin-vinaigrette mixture. Taste and season with salt and pepper if needed.

+ Divide the salad greens among 4 plates and top with the chicken salad. Serve immediately.

Stuffed Chicken Thighs

Boneless chicken thighs are a natural for stuffing, but flattening them before grilling helps them cook more quickly and evenly. Accompany these with pasta topped with a simple tomato sauce and some sautéed zucchini.

SERVES 4

$^{1}/_{2}$ cup chopped prosciutto, about 3 ounces (90 g)

$^{1}/_{2}$ cup (2 oz/60 g) shredded fontina cheese

2 teaspoons chopped fresh sage, plus 6 sage leaves

$^{1}/_{4}$ cup (1 oz/30 g) unseasoned dry breadcrumbs

$^{1}/_{4}$ cup (1 oz/30 g) freshly grated Parmesan cheese

8 boneless skinless chicken thighs

1 tablespoon olive oil

✦ In a bowl, stir together the prosciutto, fontina cheese, and chopped sage. In another bowl, combine the breadcrumbs and Parmesan.

✦ Open the chicken thighs flat and place them between two sheets of plastic wrap; pound firmly with a heavy pan or rolling pin to flatten.

✦ Preheat a two-sided electric indoor grill.

✦ Place some of the prosciutto mixture over one half of each thigh and fold the other half firmly on top. Brush the chicken with olive oil, then dip in the breadcrumb mixture.

✦ Place the chicken on the grill, setting a sage leaf on top of each piece. Close the cover and cook, in batches as necessary, until the chicken is no longer pink in the center, about 5 minutes. Serve immediately.

Blackened Chicken with Tomato-Chili Sauce

Searing the spice mixture on the outside of the chicken breasts creates a fair amount of smoke. so be sure your exhaust fan is on high if you cook this in a grill pan.

SERVES 4

For the sauce

$^1/_3$ cup (2$^1/_2$ fl oz/80 ml) tomato sauce

1 tomato, finely chopped

1 tablespoon plus 1 teaspoon fresh lime juice

1 tablespoon plus 1 teaspoon prepared chili sauce

2 teaspoons chopped fresh dill

$^1/_2$ teaspoon salt

$^1/_2$ teaspoon hot pepper sauce

Freshly ground black pepper

For the chicken

1 tablespoon plus 1 teaspoon mild paprika

2 teaspoons garlic powder

2 teaspoons onion powder

2 teaspoons freshly ground black pepper

1 teaspoon salt

1 teaspoon dried thyme leaves

$^1/_2$ teaspoon cayenne pepper

4 boneless, skinless chicken breast halves, about 1 pound (500 g) total

4 tablespoons (125 g) butter, melted

✦ To make the sauce, in a small bowl stir together all the sauce ingredients. Let the mixture stand for at least 1 hour to blend the flavors.

✦ To prepare the chicken, in a small bowl or screw-top jar combine the paprika, garlic powder, onion powder, black pepper, salt, thyme, and cayenne pepper; stir or shake thoroughly. (The spice mix can be made several weeks ahead and stored in an airtight jar at room temperature.) Transfer the mixture to a plate.

✦ Preheat a two-sided electric indoor grill or ridged grill pan according to the manufacturer's instructions.

✦ Meanwhile, place the chicken breasts between two sheets of plastic wrap and pound them with a heavy pan or rolling pin to flatten. Dip both sides of each piece in melted butter and then into the spice mixture.

✦ **If you are using the two-sided grill,** place the chicken on the grill, close the cover, and cook until the chicken is no longer pink in the center, 4 to 5 minutes.

✦ **If you are using the grill pan,** cook until the chicken is no longer pink in the center, 8 to 10 minutes, turning it once midway through the cooking time.

✦ Serve the chicken with the sauce spooned over or on the side.

Chicken Teriyaki Skewers

Serve this classic Japanese dish with white rice and pickled ginger.

SERVES 4

For the marinade

1 cup (8 fl oz/250 ml) orange juice

^{2}/$_3$ cup (5 fl oz/160 ml) dry sherry

^{1}/$_2$ cup (4 fl oz/125 ml) soy sauce

4 teaspoons sugar

2 teaspoons grated orange zest

1^1/$_2$ teaspoons grated fresh ginger

2 cloves garlic, minced

For the chicken

1 pound (500 g) boneless, skinless chicken breasts, cut into 1-inch (2.5-cm) cubes

6 scallions, trimmed and cut into 1^1/$_2$-inch (4-cm) pieces

+ To make the marinade, in a small bowl combine the orange juice, sherry, soy sauce, sugar, orange zest, ginger, and garlic. Reserve $2/3$ cup (5 fl oz/ 160 ml) and pour the rest into a long, shallow, nonreactive baking dish.

+ Thread the chicken onto skewers alternately with the scallions, leaving a little space between the pieces. Place in the marinade and turn to coat. Let stand at room temperature for 30 minutes, turning the skewers from time to time.

+ Meanwhile, place the reserved $2/3$ cup (5 fl oz/160 ml) marinade in a small saucepan and simmer until thickened slightly, about 5 minutes. Set aside.

+ Preheat a two-sided electric indoor grill or ridged grill pan according to the manufacturer's instructions.

+ Remove the skewers from the marinade, shaking off the excess. Discard the used marinade.

+ **If you are using the two-sided grill,** place the skewers on the grill, close the cover, and cook, in batches as necessary, until the chicken is no longer pink in the center, 2 to 3 minutes.

+ **If you are using the grill pan**, cook the skewers, in batches as necessary, until the chicken is no longer pink in the center, 4 to 6 minutes, turning once midway through the cooking time.

+ Place the skewers on a platter, brush with the reserved cooked marinade, and serve immediately.

Grilled Chicken Breasts with Walnut-Sage Pesto

This chicken goes nicely with garlic mashed potatoes. The recipe makes more pesto than you'll need—serve leftovers tossed with pasta and roasted butternut squash or spread the pesto onto grilled country bread for extraordinary chicken sandwiches.

SERVES 4

For the pesto

1^1/$_2$ cups (6 oz/185 g) walnuts

^{1}/$_2$ cup (2 oz/60 g) freshly grated Parmesan cheese

2 teaspoons chopped fresh sage

2 cloves garlic

^{1}/$_4$ teaspoon salt

Freshly ground black pepper

6 tablespoons (3 fl oz/90 ml) extra-virgin olive oil

For the chicken

2 teaspoons olive oil

4 boneless, skinless chicken breast halves, about 1 pound (500 g) total

Salt and freshly ground black pepper

4 teaspoons chopped fresh parsley

photograph on page 52

64

◆ Preheat the oven to 350°F (180°C). Place the walnuts on a baking sheet and bake until nicely toasted, about 10 minutes. Let cool.

◆ To make the pesto, place the walnuts, Parmesan cheese, sage, garlic, salt, and several grinds of pepper in a food processor and pulse until the nuts are coarsely ground. Add the olive oil and pulse just until blended, scraping down the sides once with a rubber spatula.

◆ Preheat a two-sided electric indoor grill or ridged grill pan according to the manufacturer's instructions.

◆ Rub olive oil over both sides of the chicken and season with salt and pepper.

◆ **If you are using the two-sided grill,** place the chicken on the grill, close the cover, and cook until the chicken is no longer pink in the center, 4 to 5 minutes.

◆ **If you are using the grill pan**, cook until the chicken is no longer pink in the center, 8 to 10 minutes, turning it once midway through the cooking time.

◆ Slice the chicken on the diagonal into ½-inch (12-mm)-thick strips. Fan out the chicken strips on 4 dinner plates and top with a dollop of pesto and a sprinkle of parsley. Serve immediately.

Middle Eastern Chicken Kabobs

To accompany the kabobs, grill skewers of red bell peppers and mushrooms brushed with olive oil and serve with pita bread.

SERVES 4

For the marinade

1 onion, chopped

4 cloves garlic, chopped

$1/4$ cup (2 fl oz/60 ml) fresh lemon juice

1 tablespoon chopped fresh thyme or $1^1/2$ teaspoons dried

1 tablespoon paprika

$1/2$ teaspoon cayenne pepper

$1/2$ teaspoon freshly ground black pepper

1 cup (8 oz/250 g) plain yogurt

For the chicken

1 pound (500 g) boneless, skinless chicken breasts, cut into 1-inch (2.5-cm) cubes

Salt and freshly ground black pepper

◆ To make the marinade, in a food processor place the onion, garlic, lemon juice, thyme, paprika, cayenne pepper, and black pepper and pulse until well combined. Add the yogurt and pulse until blended. Pour the marinade into a nonreactive bowl or dish. Add the chicken to the marinade and turn to coat. Cover and refrigerate for 6 to 8 hours.

◆ Preheat a two-sided electric indoor grill or ridged grill pan according to the manufacturer's instructions.

◆ Remove the chicken pieces from the marinade and wipe off the excess.

◆ **If you are using the two-sided grill,** thread the chicken onto skewers, leaving a little space between the pieces. Sprinkle with salt and pepper. Place the skewers on the grill, close the cover, and cook, in batches as necessary, until the chicken is no longer pink in the center, 2 to 3 minutes.

◆ **If you are using the grill pan**, thread the chicken onto skewers, leaving a little space between the pieces. Sprinkle with salt and pepper. Cook, in batches as necessary, until the chicken is no longer pink in the center, 4 to 6 minutes, turning once midway through the cooking time.

◆ Serve immediately.

Pecan-Crusted Chicken Breasts with Sherried Peaches

The sweet-sour peach sauce is a beautiful topping for the nutty chicken breasts, but the chicken is also delicious on its own.

SERVES 4

For the peaches

2 peaches, peeled and sliced, about 2 cups
(12 oz/ 375 g), or frozen sliced peaches, thawed

2 tablespoons sugar

1 tablespoon dry sherry

1 tablespoon sherry vinegar or cider vinegar

For the chicken

$1^{1}/_{3}$ cups (5 oz/160 g) pecan halves

$^{1}/_{2}$ teaspoon dried thyme leaves

$^{1}/_{2}$ teaspoon salt

$^{1}/_{4}$ teaspoon freshly ground black pepper

$1^{1}/_{2}$ tablespoons Dijon mustard

$1^{1}/_{2}$ tablespoons olive oil

4 boneless, skinless chicken breast halves,
about 1 pound (500 g) total

+ To prepare the peaches, in a saucepan combine the peaches, sugar, sherry, and vinegar; bring to a simmer over medium heat and cook until the peaches are tender and the juices have thickened, about 10 minutes. Cover and set aside to keep warm.

+ To prepare the chicken, in a food processor combine the pecans, thyme, salt, and pepper and process until the nuts are finely ground. Transfer the mixture to a plate.

+ In a small bowl, stir together the mustard and oil until well combined.

+ Place the chicken breasts between two sheets of plastic wrap, and pound with a heavy pan or rolling pin to flatten them.

+ Preheat a two-sided electric indoor grill according to the manufacturer's instructions.

+ Using the back of a spoon, spread 1 teaspoon of the mustard-oil mixture over one side of a chicken breast; place it coated side down on top of the pecan mixture. Spread the second side with another teaspoon of the mustard mixture and turn to coat the second side with nuts. Repeat coating for the remaining chicken.

+ Place the chicken on the grill, close the cover, and cook until the chicken is no longer pink in the center, 4 to 5 minutes.

+ Serve topped with the warm sherried peaches.

Chicken Cacciatore on the Grill

Whole garlic cloves become soft and mellow on the grill right alongside the chicken, adding a rich flavor to this fastest-ever "hunter-style" Italian classic. Serve it on a bed of pasta, rice, or polenta.

SERVES 4

1 cut-up frying chicken, about 4 pounds (2 kg)

1 yellow onion, thinly sliced

1 green bell pepper, seeded and thinly sliced

1 stalk celery, thinly sliced

3 whole cloves garlic, unpeeled

1 tablespoon olive oil

1 (28 oz/875 g) can chopped tomatoes

$^{1}/_{4}$ cup (2 fl oz/60 ml) dry white wine

$^{1}/_{2}$ teaspoon sugar

Salt and freshly ground black pepper

photograph on page 53

+ Rinse the chicken pieces and pat dry. Reserve the wings for another use.

+ Preheat a large two-sided electric indoor grill according to the manufacturer's instructions.

+ In a small bowl, toss the onion, pepper, celery, and garlic with the oil. Arrange the chicken skin side down over two-thirds of the grill. Remove the garlic cloves from the vegetable mixture and place them in the open area of the grill, spooning the remaining vegetables on top. Close the cover and cook for 8 minutes.

+ Give the vegetables a toss, making sure the garlic cloves remain at the bottom, and continue cooking until the chicken is no longer pink in the center and the vegetables are browned and tender, about 7 minutes.

+ Transfer the chicken to a serving platter and cover to keep it warm.

+ Scrape the cooked vegetables into a medium saucepan, setting the garlic cloves aside. Add the tomatoes, wine, and sugar to the saucepan and bring to a simmer over medium-high heat.

+ Meanwhile, squeeze the softened garlic from the skins and with the flat side of a knife mash it into a paste. Add the garlic paste to the tomato mixture and cook until the mixture is reduced and thickened, about 5 minutes. Season with salt and pepper to taste.

+ Spoon the sauce over the chicken and serve while hot.

Jerk Chicken Kabobs with Banana-Ginger Chutney

Serve these Caribbean-inspired kabobs with black beans and rice. The chutney can be made a day ahead and refrigerated, but be sure to bring it to room temperature before serving.

SERVES 4

For the chicken

1 pound (500 g) boneless, skinless chicken breasts, cut into 1^{1}/$_{2}$-inch (4-cm) pieces

^{1}/$_{4}$ cup (2 oz/60 g) prepared jerk seasoning

For the chutney

1 tablespoon canola oil

1 shallot, thinly sliced

1 jalapeño chile, seeded and minced

1 tablespoon minced fresh ginger

2 large almost-ripe bananas, peeled, halved lengthwise and cut across into ^{1}/$_{4}$-inch (6-mm) pieces

^{1}/$_{2}$ cup (3^{1}/$_{2}$ oz/105 g) brown sugar

^{1}/$_{2}$ cup (4 fl oz/125 ml) orange juice

^{1}/$_{4}$ cup (2 fl oz/60 ml) cider vinegar

^{1}/$_{2}$ teaspoon ground coriander

Large pinch of cayenne pepper

^{1}/$_{2}$ teaspoon salt

Freshly ground black pepper

2 tablespoons fresh lime juice

✦ In a small, shallow, nonreactive dish coat the chicken with the jerk seasoning. Cover and refrigerate for 1 to 2 hours.

✦ To make the chutney, in a medium saucepan heat the canola oil over medium heat. Add the shallot and cook, stirring often, for 2 minutes. Add the jalapeño and ginger and cook, stirring, for $1^{1}/_{2}$ minutes more. Add the bananas, brown sugar, orange juice, vinegar, coriander, cayenne pepper, salt, and black pepper to taste, and stir to combine. Bring to a boil, lower the heat, and simmer, stirring occasionally, until thickened, about 10 minutes. Remove from the heat and stir in the lime juice.

✦ Preheat a two-sided electric indoor grill or ridged grill pan according to the manufacturer's instructions.

✦ **If you are using the two-sided grill,** thread the chicken onto skewers, leaving a little space between the pieces. Place the skewers on the grill, close the cover, and cook, in batches as necessary, until the chicken is no longer pink in the center, 2 to 3 minutes.

✦ **If you are using the grill pan,** thread the chicken onto skewers, leaving a little space between the pieces. Cook, in batches as necessary, until the chicken is no longer pink in the center, 4 to 6 minutes, turning once midway through the cooking time.

✦ Serve immediately, passing the chutney separately.

Chicken Breasts Stuffed with Tomato-Mint Pesto

This simple recipe has great flavor and sophistication, making it perfect for a dinner party. Serve the chicken with roasted asparagus or green beans and orzo tossed with olive oil and parsley.

SERVES 4

For the pesto

5 sun-dried tomatoes, packed in oil

2 tablespoons packed fresh mint leaves

2 tablespoons packed fresh parsley leaves

1 clove garlic, halved

$1/2$ teaspoon grated lemon zest

$1/2$ teaspoon salt, plus more as needed

$1/8$ teaspoon freshly ground black pepper, plus more as needed

$1/4$ cup (2 fl oz/60 ml) extra-virgin olive oil

For the chicken

2 teaspoons olive oil

4 boneless, skinless chicken breast halves, about 1 pound (500 g) total

◆ To make the pesto, in a food processor or blender, combine all the pesto ingredients. Process until the mixture forms a thick paste, stopping to scrape down the sides of the bowl from time to time. Season with salt and pepper to taste.

◆ To prepare the chicken, using a paring knife, cut a slit about 2 to 2½ inches (5 cm) long down the rounded side of each chicken breast. Open the slit through the chicken horizontally to create a pocket, taking care not to cut through the other side. Fill each pocket with one-quarter of the pesto.

◆ Preheat a two-sided electric indoor grill or ridged grill pan according to the manufacturer's instructions.

◆ Rub the remaining 2 teaspoons olive oil over both sides of the chicken and season with salt and pepper.

◆ **If you are using the two-sided grill,** place the chicken on the grill, close the cover, and cook until the chicken is no longer pink in the center, 4 to 5 minutes.

◆ **If you are using the grill pan,** cook until the chicken is no longer pink in the center, 8 to 10 minutes, turning it once midway through the cooking time.

◆ Serve immediately.

Chicken Thighs
with Quick Mole Sauce

Mole (MO-lay) means "concoction," and there are limitless variations on this classic rich Mexican sauce, which is usually slow-simmered. This fast version is great served with rice and a salad of greens, red onion, and sliced oranges.

SERVES 3 TO 4

For the sauce

2 tablespoons vegetable oil

$^1/_2$ cup (2 oz/60 g) sliced almonds

1 onion, chopped

2 cloves garlic, chopped

$^1/_2$ teaspoon salt

3 tablespoons chili powder

$^1/_4$ teaspoon ground cinnamon

$^1/_4$ teaspoon ground coriander

$^1/_8$ teaspoon ground cloves

1 (8 fl oz/250 ml) can tomato sauce

$^3/_4$ cup (6 fl oz/180 ml) chicken broth

$^1/_2$ small corn tortilla, torn into pieces

$^1/_4$ cup (1$^1/_2$ oz/45 g) raisins

1 ounce (30 g) bittersweet (not semisweet) chocolate, coarsely chopped

For the chicken

6 bone-in chicken thighs, trimmed of excess fat

Salt and freshly ground black pepper

✦ To make the sauce, in a medium skillet heat 1 tablespoon of the oil over medium-high heat. Add the almonds and cook, stirring, until golden and toasted, about 3 minutes; transfer to a blender or food processor.

✦ Add the onion and the remaining 1 tablespoon oil to the skillet; reduce the heat to medium and cook, stirring, until the onions are softened, about 5 minutes.

✦ In a small bowl, mash the garlic and salt together to make a paste. Add the paste to the softened onions, along with the chili powder, cinnamon, coriander, and cloves; cook until fragrant, about 2 minutes more.

✦ Add the onion mixture to the almonds in the blender or food processor. Add the tomato sauce, chicken broth, and tortilla pieces and blend until smooth. Return the mixture to the skillet and add the raisins and chocolate; stir over medium heat until the chocolate is melted.

✦ Preheat a large two-sided electric indoor grill or ridged grill pan according to the manufacturer's instructions.

✦ Season both sides of the chicken thighs with salt and pepper.

✦ **If you are using the two-sided grill,** place the chicken on the grill, close the cover, and cook until the chicken is no longer pink next to the bone, 8 to 10 minutes.

✦ **If you are using the grill pan,** cook until the chicken is no longer pink next to the bone, 15 to 20 minutes, turning it once midway through the cooking time.

✦ Rewarm the sauce and spoon over the chicken.

Chicken Satay

A favorite dish in Indonesia, satays are skewers of marinated cubes or strips of meat, fish, or poultry, which are grilled and served with a spicy peanut sauce.
For indoor grilling, use chicken tenders and grill them before threading the skewers.

SERVES 4

For the satay sauce

2 tablespoons light brown sugar

1 tablespoon sesame oil

1 clove garlic, minced

1 tablespoon minced fresh ginger

$1/4$–$1/2$ teaspoon crushed red pepper flakes

$1/2$ cup (4 oz/125 g) peanut butter

$1/4$ cup (2 oz/60 g) ketchup

3 tablespoons water

1 tablespoon rice wine vinegar

1 tablespoon soy sauce

1 tablespoon fresh lime juice

For the chicken

12 chicken tenders, about $1^1/4$ pounds (625 g) total, tendons and fat trimmed

1 tablespoon sesame oil, preferably dark

Salt and freshly ground black pepper

◆ To make the sauce, in a small saucepan combine the brown sugar, sesame oil, garlic, ginger, and red pepper flakes. Cook over low heat, stirring constantly, until fragrant, about 2 minutes. Remove from the heat. Add the peanut butter, ketchup, water, vinegar, soy sauce, and lime juice. Whisk until smooth. Set aside. (The sauce will keep, covered, in the refrigerator for up to 2 weeks.)

◆ To prepare the chicken, in a medium bowl combine the chicken and sesame oil. Season with salt and pepper to taste.

◆ Preheat a two-sided electric indoor grill or ridged grill pan according to the manufacturer's instructions.

◆ **If you are using the two-sided grill,** place the chicken tenders on the grill, close the cover, and cook until the chicken is no longer pink in the center, 2 to 3 minutes.

◆ **If you are using the grill pan,** cook until the chicken is no longer pink in the center, 4 to 6 minutes, turning it once midway through the cooking time.

◆ Thread each piece of chicken lengthwise onto a 12-inch bamboo skewer. Serve the skewers with the satay sauce for dipping.

Five-Spice Cornish Hens with Dipping Sauce

Equally delicious served cold, this dish makes perfect picnic fare. The dipping sauce, a common condiment on Vietnamese and Thai tables, can be used with many dishes, such as spring rolls and grilled fish.

For the hens

2 Rock Cornish hens, $1^3/4$ pounds (875 g) each
1-inch (2.5-cm) piece ginger, peeled and grated
4 cloves garlic, chopped
2 shallots, chopped
$1^1/2$ tablespoons brown sugar
2 tablespoons Vietnamese or Thai fish sauce
2 tablespoons soy sauce
1 tablespoon dry sherry
$1/2$ teaspoon Chinese five-spice powder
$1/4$ teaspoon freshly ground black pepper

For the sauce

$1/4$ cup (2 oz/60 g) sugar
1 small fresh hot red chile, seeded and finely chopped
1 clove garlic, finely chopped
$1/2$ cup (4 fl oz/125 ml) water
$1/3$ cup (3 fl oz/90 ml) Vietnamese or Thai fish sauce
$1/4$ cup (2 fl oz/60 ml) fresh lime juice

◆ To prepare the hens, rinse them inside and out and pat dry. With a large chef's knife, cut each hen in half through the breast and backbone.

◆ In a blender or mini food processor, combine the ginger, garlic, shallots, and brown sugar; process to a paste. Add the fish sauce, soy sauce, sherry, five-spice powder, and pepper; process to combine.

◆ Transfer the marinade to a shallow, nonreactive dish; add the hens, and turn to coat them. Cover and refrigerate for 4 to 12 hours, turning occasionally.

◆ To make the sauce, using a mortar and pestle mash the sugar, chile, and garlic to a paste. Transfer the paste to a small bowl and add the water, fish sauce, and lime juice. Stir until the sugar is dissolved.

◆ Strain the sauce into a bowl or jar and use immediately, or refrigerate, tightly covered, for up to 5 days.

◆ Preheat a large two-sided electric indoor grill or ridged grill pan according to the manufacturer's instructions.

◆ Remove the hens from the marinade, shaking off the excess.

◆ **If you are using the two-sided grill,** place the hens skin side down on the grill, close the cover, and cook until there are no red juices next to the bone, 15 to 18 minutes.

◆ **If you are using the grill pan,** cook the hens until there are no red juices next to the bone, 20 to 22 minutes, turning them once midway through the cooking time.

◆ Serve hot or cold with the dipping sauce.

Curried Turkey Burgers with Chutney-Yogurt Sauce

Here's a low-fat alternative to the hamburger. Serve these spicy sandwiches with roasted sweet potato wedges and coleslaw.

Serves 4

For the burgers

2 teaspoons olive oil

1 small onion, diced

1 clove garlic, minced

$1/2$ Granny Smith apple, peeled, cored, and diced

1 tablespoon curry powder

1 pound (500 g) ground turkey breast

1 teaspoon salt

$1/2$ teaspoon freshly ground black pepper

2 tablespoons chopped fresh parsley

4 pita bread rounds

4 lettuce leaves, torn into pieces

For the sauce

$3/4$ cup (6 oz/190 g) plain yogurt

$2^1/2$ tablespoons hot mango chutney

+ In a medium nonstick skillet, heat the olive oil over medium heat. Add the onion and cook, stirring occasionally, for 2 minutes. Add the garlic, apple, and curry powder and cook, stirring often, until the onion and apple are softened, 4 to 5 minutes. Let cool.

+ Preheat a two-sided electric indoor grill or ridged grill pan according to the manufacturer's instructions.

+ Place the turkey in a mixing bowl. Add the cooled onion mixture, salt, pepper, and parsley. Using your hands, mix gently but thoroughly. Form into four 1-inch (2.5-cm)-thick burgers.

+ **If you are using the two-sided grill,** place the burgers on the grill, close the cover, and cook until the burgers are just cooked through, about 6 minutes.

+ **If you are using the grill pan,** cook until the burgers are just cooked through, about 12 minutes, turning them once midway through the cooking time.

+ While the burgers are cooking, in a small bowl, stir together the yogurt and chutney. Trim $1\frac{1}{2}$ inches off the top of the pita breads and toast them.

+ Stuff a burger into each pita pocket and top with the yogurt sauce and lettuce. Serve immediately.

Turkey Breast
with Spinach-Couscous Stuffing

If you can't find a boneless turkey breast, buy a whole one and have the butcher bone it for you. Oven-roasted eggplant and tomatoes would be good complements to the Middle Eastern flavors of the turkey.

Serves 6

For the turkey

1 boneless, skinless turkey breast half, about 2 pounds
    (1 kg)
Olive oil
Salt and freshly ground black pepper

For the stuffing

8 cups (8 oz/240 g) fresh spinach leaves, thoroughly
    dried, washed, and stemmed
$^{1}/_{2}$ cup (4 fl oz/125 ml) water
$^{1}/_{3}$ cup (2 oz/60 g) instant couscous
2 tablespoons olive oil
$^{1}/_{4}$ cup (1 oz/30 g) pine nuts
1 teaspoon minced garlic
$^{1}/_{2}$ teaspoon salt, plus more as needed
$^{1}/_{4}$ teaspoon freshly ground black pepper
1 teaspoon fresh lemon juice
$^{1}/_{2}$ teaspoon grated lemon zest
1 large egg, lightly beaten

photograph on page 55

- ✦ Place the turkey smooth side up on a work surface. Trim away any fat. Cover with plastic wrap and pound with a heavy pan or rolling pin to flatten the turkey into a more even layer. (If the small tenderloin separates, don't worry, as it will meld back together during cooking.) With a knife held parallel to the work surface, and working from the thinner toward the thicker edge, cut a pocket as you would for a stuffed chicken breast, leaving the thicker edge intact. Fold the breast open for stuffing.

- ✦ To make the stuffing, coarsely chop the spinach and set aside. In a small saucepan, bring the water to a boil. Stir in the couscous, remove from the heat, cover, and let stand for 3 minutes. Fluff the couscous with a fork.

- ✦ In a large skillet, heat the olive oil over medium heat. Add the pine nuts and cook, stirring, until they begin to color, about 30 seconds. Add the garlic and continue to stir until the nuts are golden and the garlic is fragrant, about 30 seconds more. Add this mixture to the couscous.

- ✦ Return the skillet to the heat and add the spinach. Stir until it is just wilted, about 2 minutes. Remove from the heat and stir in the salt, pepper, lemon juice, lemon zest, and the reserved couscous mixture. Stir in the egg.

- ✦ Preheat a large two-sided electric indoor grill according to the manufacturer's instructions.

- ✦ Spread the stuffing over half of the turkey breast in an even layer. Fold the top half firmly over the filling. Rub the top with olive oil and season with salt and pepper.

- ✦ Place the turkey on the grill, close the cover, and cook until it is no longer pink in the center, about 8 minutes.

- ✦ Slide the turkey onto a cutting board or serving dish and let it stand for a few minutes. Cut it crosswise into wide slices and serve.

Grilled Duck Breasts
with Cranberry-Pear Compote

Roasted acorn squash, sliced and drizzled with hazelnut oil, makes an elegant accompaniment to this festive dish.

SERVES 4

For the compote

2 teaspoons canola oil

1 large shallot, minced

$1^1/2$ teaspoons chopped fresh rosemary

2 cups (8 oz/250 g) fresh or frozen cranberries

$^1/3$ cup (2 oz/60 g) diced dried pears

1 cup (8 fl oz/250 ml) water

$^1/2$ cup ($3^1/2$ oz/105 g) brown sugar

1 tablespoon balsamic vinegar

Freshly ground black pepper

For the duck

2 teaspoons olive oil

4 boneless duck breast halves, about $1^1/2$ pounds (750 g) total

Salt and freshly ground black pepper

photograph on page 54

✦ To make the compote, in a medium saucepan heat the canola oil over medium-high heat. Add the shallot and sauté until softened, about 3 minutes. Stir in the rosemary and cook, stirring, about 30 seconds more. Stir in the remaining compote ingredients and bring the mixture to a boil. Lower the heat slightly and boil, stirring often, for 10 minutes. Set aside.

✦ Preheat a two-sided electric indoor grill or ridged grill pan according to the manufacturer's instructions.

✦ Rub olive oil over both sides of the duck breasts and season with salt and pepper.

✦ **If you are using the two-sided grill,** place the duck breasts on the grill, close the cover, and cook to the desired degree of doneness, about 4 minutes for medium rare.

✦ **If you are using the grill pan,** place the duck on the pan skin side down, and cook until it is well browned on the bottom, about 6 minutes. Turn and cook to the desired degree of doneness, 2 to 3 minutes more for medium rare.

✦ Divide among 4 plates and spoon the compote over and around the duck. Serve immediately.

Beef

Deluxe Sirloin Burgers

Vegetables tossed with a light lemon vinaigrette offer a refreshing counterpoint to mildly spiced sirloin patties.

<small>SERVES 4</small>

1^1/$_2$ tablespoons fresh lemon juice

^{1}/$_4$ cup (2 fl oz/60 ml) extra-virgin olive oil

4 thick slices tomato

4 thick slices red onion

1 teaspoon salt, plus more as needed

^{1}/$_2$ teaspoon freshly ground black pepper, plus more as needed

1 pound (500 g) ground sirloin

^{1}/$_3$ cup (2^1/$_2$ fl oz/80 ml) prepared chili sauce

2 tablespoons ice water

4 large onion rolls or hamburger buns

1 cup shredded iceberg lettuce

photograph on page 129

+ In a shallow, nonreactive dish, combine the lemon juice and 3 tablespoons of the olive oil. Add the tomato and onion and turn to coat. Season with salt and pepper to taste and set aside.

+ Preheat a two-sided electric indoor grill or ridged grill pan according to the manufacturer's instructions.

+ In a mixing bowl, combine the ground sirloin, salt, pepper, chili sauce, and ice water. Mix well. Using your hands, gently form the mixture into four 1-inch (2.5 cm)-thick hamburger patties.

+ **If you are using the two-sided grill,** place the burgers on the grill, close the cover, and cook to the desired degree of doneness, 4 to 7 minutes for medium.

+ **If you are using the grill pan,** cook the burgers to the desired degree of doneness, 8 to 14 minutes for medium, turning them once midway through the cooking time.

+ Toast the buns, then brush the cut sides with the remaining olive oil. Place each burger on the bottom half of a bun, top with a slice of tomato and onion, and a quarter of the lettuce. Serve immediately.

Thai Beef Salad

SERVES 4

For the beef

2 cloves garlic

2 tablespoons finely chopped cilantro

1$^{1}/_{2}$ teaspoons sugar

1 teaspoon freshly ground black pepper

2 tablespoons soy sauce

1 tablespoon Thai fish sauce

1 tablespoon peanut or corn oil

1 pound (500 g) boneless sirloin steak

For the vinaigrette and salad

2 cloves garlic, minced

2 small fresh red or green chiles, chopped

1$^{1}/_{2}$ tablespoons sugar

$^{1}/_{4}$ cup (2 fl oz/60 ml) Thai fish sauce

$^{1}/_{3}$ cup (3 fl oz/80 ml) fresh lime juice

6 large red lettuce leaves, torn into pieces

3 small firm tomatoes, cut into wedges

1 small red onion, thinly sliced

1 small cucumber, peeled and thinly sliced

2 tablespoons coarsely chopped cilantro, plus whole leaves for garnish

2 tablespoons coarsely chopped fresh mint

✦ To prepare the beef, use a mortar and pestle and combine the garlic, cilantro, sugar, and pepper; mash to a paste. Stir in the soy sauce, fish sauce, and oil. Place the beef in a shallow dish and rub the mixture over both sides. Marinate for 1 hour at room temperature or cover and refrigerate for up to 4 hours.

✦ To make the vinaigrette, use a mortar and pestle and combine the garlic and chilies; mash to a paste. Stir in the sugar, fish sauce, and lime juice. Set aside.

✦ Preheat a two-sided electric indoor grill or ridged grill pan according to the manufacturer's instructions.

✦ **If you are using the two-sided grill,** place the beef on the grill, close the cover, and cook to the desired degree of doneness, 4 to 5 minutes for medium rare. Set aside to cool.

✦ **If you are using the grill pan,** cook the beef to the desired degree of doneness, 8 to 10 minutes for medium rare, turning it once midway through the cooking time. Set aside to cool.

✦ To assemble: In a large bowl, toss the salad ingredients together with $2\frac{1}{2}$ tablespoons of the vinaigrette. Thinly slice beef across the grain, place the slices in a bowl, and toss with the remaining vinaigrette. Divide the salad among 4 plates and mound the beef mixture on top. Garnish with cilantro leaves and serve immediately.

photograph on page 131

Grilled Steak
in Red Wine Marinade

Tarragon or rosemary can replace the thyme in this recipe; use fresh if possible. This steak can be served with almost anything. For a simple approach, try corn on the cob and Old-Fashioned Potato Salad (page 234).

<small>SERVES 4</small>

For the marinade

$^1/_3$ cup (3 fl oz/80 ml) olive oil

$^1/_3$ cup (3 fl oz/80 ml) dry red wine

$^1/_2$ small yellow onion, sliced

1 tablespoon balsamic vinegar

2 cloves garlic, chopped

1 teaspoon salt

$^1/_2$ teaspoon freshly ground black pepper

$1^1/_2$ teaspoons chopped fresh thyme,
or $^1/_2$ teaspoon dried

For the steak

$1–1^1/_2$ pounds (500–750 g) boneless sirloin steak,
cut $1–1^1/_4$ inches (2.5–3 cm) thick

♦ To make the marinade, in a small bowl combine all the marinade ingredients and whisk to combine.

♦ Place the steak in a large resealable plastic bag or shallow, nonreactive dish; pour in the marinade and turn the steak to coat it. Cover the dish, if using, and refrigerate for at least 2 hours or overnight.

♦ Preheat a two-sided electric indoor grill or ridged grill pan according to the manufacturer's instructions.

♦ Remove the steak from the marinade, shaking off the excess.

♦ **If you are using the two-sided grill,** place the steak on the grill, close the cover, and cook to the desired degree of doneness, 4 to 5 minutes for a 1-inch (2.5-cm)-thick steak cooked to medium rare.

♦ **If you are using the grill pan,** cook the steak to the desired degree of doneness, 8 to 10 minutes for a 1-inch (2.5-cm)-thick steak cooked to medium rare, turning it once midway through the cooking time.

♦ Transfer the steak to a platter and let it stand for a few minutes before serving.

Grilled Beef Tacos

With family or friends, it's hard to beat the fun of this hands-on favorite. The recipe calls for soft tacos, but you could also use crisp taco shells if you prefer.

SERVES 4

For the garnishes

$1/4$ head iceberg lettuce, shredded

2 avocados, pitted, peeled, diced, tossed gently with 2 tablespoons lime juice

2 tomatoes, seeded and diced

4 scallions, sliced, including green tops

2 tablespoons coarsely chopped fresh cilantro

Quick Tomato Salsa (page 25) or purchased tomato salsa

For the beef

8 large corn tortillas

1 pound (500 g) skirt or flank steak

Salt and freshly ground black pepper

2 cloves garlic, minced

1 tablespoon olive oil

1 tablespoon fresh lime juice

photograph on page 134

✦ Prepare all the garnishes, place them in serving bowls, and set aside.

✦ Preheat the oven to 300°F (150°C). Preheat a large two-sided electric indoor grill or ridged grill pan according to the manufacturer's instructions.

✦ Directly on top of electric or gas stove burners, lightly toast both sides of the tortillas. Wrap them in foil and keep them warm in the oven.

✦ Season both sides of the steak with salt and pepper. Rub both sides with the minced garlic, then with the olive oil, and drizzle both sides with the lime juice.

✦ **If you are using the two-sided grill,** place the steak on the grill, close the cover, and cook to the desired degree of doneness, 4 to 5 minutes for medium rare.

✦ **If you are using the grill pan,** cook the steak to the desired degree of doneness, 8 minutes for medium rare, turning it once midway through the cooking time.

✦ Transfer the steak to a cutting board and let it stand for 5 minutes. Cut across the grain into $1/4$-inch (6-mm)-thick slices. Serve with the warmed tortillas and garnishes, letting everyone assemble his or her own tacos.

Steak Kabobs

Because beef for kabobs has more surface area, it doesn't need as long to absorb the flavors of a marinade. Serve these over rice cooked with a little lemon juice and zest.

SERVES 4

For the marinade

1/4 cup (2 fl oz/60 ml) olive oil

1 tablespoon fresh lemon juice

6 cloves garlic, sliced

For the kabobs

1 pound (500 g) boneless sirloin steak, cut into 1 1/4-inch (3-cm) cubes

2 bunches scallions, cut into 2-inch (5-cm) lengths

16 cherry tomatoes

Salt and freshly ground black pepper

✦ To make the marinade, in a small bowl whisk together the oil, lemon juice, and garlic. Place the steak cubes in a large resealable plastic bag or shallow, nonreactive dish; pour in the marinade and toss to coat the meat. Cover the dish, if using. Refrigerate for 1 to 2 hours.

✦ Remove the meat from the marinade, shaking off the excess. Thread the cubes onto skewers, alternating with pieces of scallion and tomatoes, leaving a little space between the pieces. Season on all sides with salt and pepper.

✦ Preheat a large two-sided electric indoor grill or ridged grill pan according to the manufacturer's instructions.

✦ **If you are using the two-sided grill,** place the kabobs on the grill, close the cover, and cook, in batches as necessary, to the desired degree of doneness, 2 to 3 minutes for medium rare.

✦ **If you are using the grill pan,** cook the kabobs, in batches as necessary, to the desired degree of doneness, 4 to 6 minutes for medium rare, turning them once midway through the cooking time.

✦ Serve at once.

Grilled Reuben Sandwich

Great for lunch on a chilly day, the classic deli sandwich gains a new twist from tart apples sautéed in cider. Serve with potato chips, coleslaw, and dill pickles.

SERVES 4

For the spread

1/2 cup (4 oz/125 g) mayonnaise (regular or reduced fat)

2 tablespoons ketchup

2 tablespoons minced red onion

2 tablespoons minced dill pickle

2 tablespoons minced fresh parsley

1/4–1/2 teaspoon chili powder (hot or mild)

Salt and freshly ground black pepper

For the sandwich

2 teaspoons canola oil

2 tart apples, peeled, cored, and thinly sliced

1/4 cup (2 fl oz/60 ml) apple cider or apple juice

1 cup drained sauerkraut

8 slices rye bread

8 slices Swiss cheese

1/2 pound (250 g) thinly sliced corned beef

✦ To make the spread, in a small bowl stir together the mayonnaise, ketchup, onions, pickles, parsley, and chili powder; season with salt and pepper to taste. (The spread will keep, covered, in the refrigerator for up to 2 days.)

✦ To make the sandwiches, in a sauté pan heat the oil over medium-high heat. Add the apples and cook, stirring, until they start to brown, 3 to 5 minutes. Add the cider and cook, stirring, until the cider has been absorbed, about 2 minutes more. Remove from the heat and stir in the sauerkraut.

✦ Arrange the bread slices in a single layer on a work surface. Spread a layer of the spread on all 8 slices and place a slice of cheese on top of each. (Be careful not to let the cheese hang over the edges of the bread.) Divide the corned beef and sauerkraut mixture among 4 of the slices and top with the remaining 4 slices of bread, cheese side down. If desired, brush with oil or lightly butter the outside of the sandwiches.

✦ Preheat a two-sided electric indoor grill or ridged grill pan according to the manufacturer's instructions.

✦ **If you are using the two-sided grill,** place 2 sandwiches on the grill, close the cover, and cook until the bread is toasted and the cheese has melted, about 3 minutes. Repeat with the remaining sandwiches.

✦ **If you are using the grill pan,** place 2 sandwiches in the pan and cook until the bread is toasted and the cheese has melted, about 6 minutes, carefully turning the sandwiches once midway through the cooking time. Repeat with the remaining sandwiches.

✦ Serve warm.

Coriander-Crusted Beef Tenderloin with Grilled Scallions

The Asian flavors of this delicious beef dish can be easily converted into an Asian noodle salad. Simply toss cooked and cooled lo mein noodles with the scallion marinade and top with the sliced beef. Cut the scallions into pieces and scatter them over the top.

SERVES 4

For the scallions

1/4 cup (2 fl oz/60 ml) fresh lime juice

2 tablespoons soy sauce

2 tablespoons canola oil

1 jalapeño chile, seeded and minced

1 teaspoon grated fresh ginger

16 scallions, trimmed to about 8 inches (20 cm)

For the beef

1 tablespoon coriander seeds

1¹/₂ teaspoons black peppercorns

1¹/₂ teaspoons coarse salt

2 teaspoons toasted sesame oil

4 beef tenderloin steaks, cut 1–1¹/₄ inches (2.5–3 cm) thick, about 1–1¹/₂ pounds (500–750 g) total

¹/₂ lime

4 teaspoons very coarsely chopped fresh cilantro

✦ To prepare the scallions, in a shallow, nonreactive dish, whisk the lime juice, soy sauce, oil, jalapeño, and ginger together. Add the scallions and turn to coat. Let stand at room temperature for about 1 hour.

✦ In a spice grinder, pulse the coriander seeds and peppercorns until coarsely cracked (or put them in a plastic bag and crack them with a rolling pin or heavy pot). Transfer to a small dish and mix in the salt. Rub the steaks on both sides with the sesame oil, then coat them with the spice mixture.

✦ Preheat a two-sided electric indoor grill or ridged grill pan according to the manufacturer's instructions.

✦ **If you are using the two-sided grill,** arrange the scallions on the grill, close the cover, and cook until they are browned and tender (turning if necessary to make grill marks on both sides), 8 to 10 minutes. Set aside and keep them warm.

Place the steaks on the grill, close the cover, and cook to the desired degree of doneness, 4 to 5 minutes for medium rare. Transfer the steaks to a cutting board and let stand for 5 minutes.

✦ **If you are using the grill pan,** cook the scallions until they are browned and tender, about 15 minutes, turning them once midway through. Set aside and keep them warm.

Cook the steaks to the desired degree of doneness, 8 to 10 minutes for medium rare, turning them once midway through the cooking time. Transfer to a cutting board and let stand for 5 minutes.

✦ Cut the steaks into $1/2$-inch (12-mm)-thick slices and squeeze the lime over the meat. Fan the slices onto 4 plates and sprinkle with the cilantro. Arrange the scallions next to the steaks and serve immediately.

Roast Beef Hash Patties

Hash makes a wonderfully simple old-fashioned supper. The traditional topping for hash is ketchup, though Horseradish Sauce (page 112) offers a nice change of pace. Corned beef can be used instead of roast beef or steak.

1 cup (4 oz/125 g) unseasoned dry breadcrumbs

4 tablespoons (2 oz/60 g) butter, melted

2 cups (16 oz/500 g) finely diced leftover cooked roast beef or steak

2 cups (16 oz/500 g) finely diced cooked potatoes

1 small onion, finely chopped

$^1/_4$ cup (2 fl oz/60 ml) cream or milk

$^1/_2$ teaspoon salt

$^1/_4$ teaspoon freshly ground black pepper

◆ In a small bowl, stir together the breadcrumbs and butter until well combined; spread out on a small plate.

◆ In another bowl, combine the beef, potatoes, onion, cream or milk, salt, and pepper. Mash the mixture with a fork until it is combined and holds together well. Shape into 4 equal patties.

◆ Preheat a two-sided electric indoor grill or ridged grill pan according to the manufacturer's instructions.

◆ Press both sides of each patty into the breadcrumbs.

◆ **If you are using the two-sided grill,** place the patties on the grill, close the cover, and cook until nicely browned, about 3 minutes.

◆ **If you are using the grill pan,** cook until the patties are nicely browned, about 6 minutes, turning them once midway through the cooking time.

◆ Serve at once.

Warm Grilled Steak & Potato Salad

*Both the steak
and the potatoes
for this hearty
salad supper are
quickly cooked on
the grill, and a
creamy Parmesan
dressing ties them
together.*

SERVES 4

For the vinaigrette

$1/3$ cup (1 oz/40 g) freshly grated Parmesan cheese

3 tablespoons cider vinegar

2 tablespoons mayonnaise (regular or reduced fat)

1 teaspoon Dijon mustard

1 small clove garlic

$1/2$ teaspoon salt

$1/4$ teaspoon freshly ground black pepper

$1/2$ cup (4 fl oz/125 ml) extra-virgin olive oil

For the salad

$1^1/2$ pounds (750 g) unpeeled red-skinned or Yukon
Gold potatoes, sliced $1/4$ inch (6 mm) thick

2 tablespoons extra-virgin olive oil

1 pound (500 g) boneless sirloin steak

8 cups romaine lettuce (about $1^1/2$ large heads),
torn into pieces

- ✦ To make the vinaigrette, in a blender or food processor combine the Parmesan cheese, vinegar, mayonnaise, mustard, garlic, salt, and pepper; blend until smooth. With the machine running, very gradually add the oil (the dressing should be creamy). Set aside.

- ✦ Preheat a large two-sided electric indoor grill or ridged grill pan according to the manufacturer's instructions.

- ✦ In a medium bowl combine the potatoes and the oil.

- ✦ **If you are using the two-sided grill,** spread the potatoes evenly over the grill, close the cover, and cook for 8 minutes. Turn and redistribute the potatoes with tongs. Continue cooking until the potatoes are tender, about 8 minutes more. Transfer them to a large bowl to cool slightly.

  Place the steak on the grill, close the cover, and cook to the desired degree of doneness, 4 to 5 minutes for medium rare. Transfer the steak to a cutting board and let it stand for a few minutes.

- ✦ **If you are using the grill pan,** spread the potatoes evenly over the pan, cover tightly with foil, and cook over medium heat, for about 15 minutes, turning once midway through. Transfer to a large bowl to cool slightly.

  Place the steak in the pan and cook to the desired degree of doneness, 8 to 10 minutes for medium rare, turning it midway through. Transfer the steak to a cutting board and let it stand for a few minutes.

- ✦ To assemble, add half of the reserved vinaigrette to the potatoes, gently turning them to coat. Make a bed of lettuce on 4 plates and top with some of the potatoes. Cut the steak across the grain into thin slices. Arrange the steak slices on top of the potatoes and drizzle with some of the remaining dressing.

Mini-Meatloaves

Perfect for a weeknight supper: all the comfort of traditional meatloaf without the lengthy wait! Microwave some new potatoes and fresh green beans to serve alongside.

SERVES 4

1 tablespoon vegetable oil

$^1/_2$ cup ($2^1/_2$ oz/75 g) minced yellow onion

1 teaspoon minced garlic

1 large egg

$^1/_4$ cup (4 fl oz/125 ml) tomato sauce

1 teaspoon Dijon mustard

1 teaspoon Worcestershire sauce

1 slice firm white bread, torn into small pieces

2 tablespoons minced fresh parsley

$^1/_2$ teaspoon salt

$^1/_4$ teaspoon freshly ground black pepper

1 pound (500 g) ground beef

4 strips bacon, cut in half

◆ In a small skillet, heat the oil over medium heat; add the onion and garlic and cook until translucent, about 3 minutes. Set the skillet aside.

◆ In a mixing bowl, whisk together the egg, tomato sauce, mustard, and Worcestershire sauce until well combined. Stir in the bread pieces and let stand for two minutes; mash with the whisk to break down the bread.

◆ Add the parsley, salt, pepper, and the reserved onion mixture and stir together well. Add the ground beef and mix together thoroughly.

◆ Preheat a two-sided electric indoor grill according to the manufacturer's instructions.

◆ With wet hands, divide the beef mixture into 4 equal parts and shape into ovals. Set two half-strips of bacon on top of each oval. Place on the grill and cook until the meat is no longer pink in the center, about 4 minutes.

Margarita Steak
with Grilled Onion Guacamole

An icy pitcher of margaritas or cold beer, along with hot corn bread and a green salad, turn this simple steak into a casual, festive dinner party.

For the steak

$^1/_3$ cup (3 fl oz/80 ml) fresh lime juice

3 tablespoons olive oil

2 tablespoons tequila

2 tablespoons triple sec liqueur

2 teaspoons sugar

1 pound (500 g) top round steak, cut 1 inch thick

Salt and freshly ground black pepper

For the guacamole

1 large red onion, cut into $^1/_2$-inch (12-mm)-thick slices

2 tablespoons extra-virgin olive oil

2 ripe avocados, pitted and peeled

1 large clove garlic, minced

1 jalapeño chile, seeded and minced

4 teaspoons fresh lime juice

1 tablespoon chopped fresh cilantro

$^1/_2$ teaspoon salt, plus more as needed

- ✦ To prepare the steak, in a shallow, nonreactive dish whisk together the lime juice, olive oil, tequila, triple sec, and sugar. Add the steak and turn to coat. Cover and refrigerate for 4 hours, turning the steak once or twice.

- ✦ Preheat a two-sided electric indoor grill or ridged grill pan according to the manufacturer's instructions.

- ✦ Remove the steak from the marinade, shaking off the excess. Season it generously on both sides with salt and pepper.

- ✦ **If you are using the two-sided grill,** coat the onions with oil, arrange them on the grill, close the cover, and cook until the onions are tender and charred, about 5 minutes. Set them aside to cool.

  Place the steak on the grill, close the cover, and cook to the desired degree of doneness, 3 to 4 minutes for medium rare. Transfer to a cutting board and let stand for 5 minutes.

- ✦ **If you are using the grill pan,** coat the onions with oil, then grill until tender and charred, 6 to 8 minutes, turning them once midway through. Set them aside to cool.

  Then cook the steak to the desired degree of doneness, 6 to 8 minutes for medium rare, turning it once midway through. Transfer to a cutting board and let stand for 5 minutes.

- ✦ While the steak is cooking, prepare the guacamole. Coarsely chop the grilled onions. In a mixing bowl, coarsely mash the avocados with a fork. Gently stir in the onions, garlic, jalapeño, lime juice, cilantro, and salt. Taste and adjust the seasoning with more salt if needed.

- ✦ To serve, thinly slice the meat across the grain, top with the guacamole, and serve immediately.

Beef Tenderloin Steaks
with Horseradish Sauce

An elegant but easy recipe for red meat fans. Serve steamed green beans, sautéed mushrooms, and garlic mashed potatoes with it. The sauce also makes a great spread on roast beef sandwiches.

SERVES 4

For the sauce

1/3 cup (3 oz/90 g) sour cream

2 tablespoons mayonnaise (regular or reduced fat)

2 tablespoons prepared horseradish

1 teaspoon fresh lemon juice plus more as needed

Salt and freshly ground black pepper

For the beef

4 beef tenderloin steaks, cut 1–1 1/4 inches (2.5–3 cm) thick, about 1–1 1/2 pounds (500–750 g) total

Olive oil, for brushing

Salt and freshly ground black pepper

photograph on page 130

✦ To make the sauce, in a small bowl combine the sour cream, mayonnaise, horseradish, and lemon juice; stir until smooth. Season with more lemon juice and salt and pepper to taste. Cover and refrigerate. (The sauce will keep in the refrigerator for up to 2 days.)

✦ Preheat a two-sided electric indoor grill or ridged grill pan according to the manufacturer's instructions.

✦ Brush both sides of the steaks with the olive oil and season them with salt and pepper.

✦ **If you are using the two-sided grill,** place the steaks on the grill, close the cover, and cook until the steaks are seared on both sides and cooked to the desired degree of doneness, 4 to 5 minutes for medium rare.

✦ **If you are using the grill pan,** sear the steaks over high heat for 2 to 3 minutes per side. Reduce the heat to medium and cook to the desired degree of doneness, 4 to 5 minutes more for medium rare, turning them once midway through the cooking time.

✦ Serve with the reserved horseradish sauce.

Ginger-Marinated London Broil

Long marination makes lean London broil more tender. as well as adding a gingery Asian bite. Serve with some oven-roasted green beans and sliced peppers. Spicy Peanut Noodles (page 236). and a hearty green salad.

SERVES 4 TO 6

For the marinade

2¹/₂-inch (6-cm) piece fresh ginger, peeled and sliced
6 cloves garlic
¹/₂ cup (4 fl oz/125 ml) dry sherry
¹/₄ cup (2 fl oz/60 ml) soy sauce
2 tablespoons rice wine vinegar
2 tablespoons vegetable oil

For the steak

1–1¹/₂ pounds (500-750 g) London broil

photograph on page 132

+ To make the marinade, in a blender or food processor pulse the ginger and garlic until coarsely chopped. Add the sherry, soy sauce, vinegar, and oil and pulse just to combine.

+ Place the steak in a large resealable plastic bag or shallow, nonreactive dish; pour in the marinade and turn the steak to coat. Cover the dish, if using, and refrigerate for at least 6 hours or overnight.

+ Preheat a two-sided electric indoor grill or ridged grill pan according to the manufacturer's instructions.

+ Remove the steak from the marinade, shaking off the excess.

+ **If you are using the two-sided grill,** place the steak on the grill, close the cover, and cook to the desired degree of doneness, about 8 minutes for medium rare for a $1\frac{1}{4}$-inch (3-cm)-thick steak.

+ **If you are using the grill pan,** cook the steak to the desired degree of doneness, about 18 minutes for medium rare for a $1\frac{1}{4}$-inch (3-cm)-thick steak, turning it once midway through the cooking time.

+ Transfer the steak to a cutting board and let stand for a few minutes before cutting it across the grain into thin slices to serve.

Blue Cheese Burgers
with Caramelized Onions

The combination of tangy blue cheese and sweet caramelized onions is a great twist on the classic hamburger. If you don't care for blue cheese, a sharp cheddar or Swiss would also work. Serve with oven-roasted potatoes, a sliced tomato salad, and coleslaw.

SERVES 4

1 tablespoon olive oil

2 onions, thinly sliced

1 teaspoon sugar

Salt and freshly ground black pepper

2 ounces blue cheese

1^{1}/4 pounds (625 g) ground sirloin

4 hamburger buns

2 cups (4 oz/120 g) fresh watercress sprigs

✦ In a large skillet, heat the oil over medium-low heat. Add the onions and sugar and cook stirring occasionally, until golden, 10 to 20 minutes. Season with salt and pepper to taste. Set the skillet aside.

✦ Cut the blue cheese into four squares about $1\frac{1}{4}$ x $1\frac{1}{4}$ x $1\frac{1}{4}$ inches (3 cm x 3 cm x 3 cm) each. Surround each square of cheese with one quarter of the ground beef and form the meat around the cheese into a patty. Season with salt and pepper.

✦ Preheat a ridged grill pan according to the manufacturer's instructions.

✦ Cook the hamburgers until they are well browned, and the cheese has melted, 8 to 10 minutes for medium, turning them once midway through the cooking time. (Use caution when flipping the burgers, so the melted cheese does not escape from the center. Do not press on the burgers during cooking.)

✦ To serve, toast the hamburger buns, and arrange the watercress, burgers, and caramelized onions on the toasted buns.

Flank Steak Pinwheels

Caesar salad and rice cooked with black beans make great south-of-the-border accompaniments for this gutsy grilled steak. When preparing flank steak, it's not recommended to cook it beyond medium rare, because it becomes much less tender.

SERVES 4

For the stuffing

2 tablespoons olive oil

1 small red bell pepper, seeded and finely chopped

1 jalapeño chile, seeded and minced

1 teaspoon minced garlic

1 teaspoon ground cumin

1 tablespoon tomato paste

1 cup (6 oz/185 g) fresh or frozen corn kernels

2 tablespoons pitted and chopped black olives, such as Kalamata

$^1/_2$ teaspoon dried oregano

$^1/_2$ teaspoon salt

For the steak

1 flank steak, about $1^1/_2$ pounds (750 g)

Salt and freshly ground black pepper

photograph on page 133

◆ To make the stuffing, in a skillet heat the olive oil over medium-high heat. Add the red pepper and the jalapeño and cook, stirring, until softened, about 3 minutes. Add the garlic and cumin and cook until fragrant, about 30 seconds more.

◆ Remove the skillet from the heat; add the tomato paste and mash it with a spoon until it is blended into the mixture. Add the corn, olives, oregano, and salt and stir together thoroughly. Set aside to cool completely.

◆ To prepare the steak, place it between two large sheets of plastic wrap. With a heavy pan or rolling pin, pound the steak into a thinner layer of even thickness.

◆ Press the corn mixture firmly and evenly over the steak. Starting with a wide edge, roll the steak and filling up together. Lightly score the top of the rolled steak to mark it into 8 equal sections. Tie a piece of cooking twine firmly around the center of each of the sections. Season the outside of the roll with salt and pepper. Cut the roll crosswise on the score marks into 8 pieces.

◆ Preheat a large two-sided electric indoor grill or ridged grill pan according to the manufacturer's instructions.

◆ **If you are using the two-sided grill,** arrange the spirals on the grill cut side down, close the cover, and cook to the desired degree of doneness, about 4 minutes for medium rare.

◆ **If you are using the grill pan,** place the spirals on the pan cut side down, and cook to the desired degree of doneness, about 7 minutes for medium rare, turning them carefully midway through the cooking time.

◆ Divide the pinwheels among 4 plates and serve.

Sirloin Steak
in Coffee-Pepper Marinade

Fresh-ground coffee and a generous dose of black pepper make an assertive, unusual, and delicious marinade for steak. A fresh spinach salad and French-fried or oven-roasted potatoes would be perfect companions for this hearty steak.

SERVES 4

For the marinade

$1/3$ cup (3 fl oz/80 ml) olive oil

$1/3$ cup (3 fl oz/80 ml) cider vinegar

$1/4$ cup (1 oz/30 g) chopped shallots

$1^{1}/2$ tablespoons freshly ground coffee

1 tablespoon freshly ground black pepper

1 teaspoon Dijon mustard

1 teaspoon salt

For the steak

$1^{1}/2$ pounds (750 g) boneless sirloin steak, trimmed of excess fat

◆ To make the marinade, in a shallow, nonreactive dish just large enough to hold the steak, combine the oil, vinegar, shallots, coffee, pepper, mustard and salt; whisk together well.

◆ Add the steak, turning to coat it. Cover tightly with plastic wrap and refrigerate for at least 6 hours or as long as overnight.

◆ Preheat a two-sided electric indoor grill or ridged grill pan according to the manufacturer's instructions.

◆ Remove the steak from the marinade, shaking off the excess.

◆ **If you are using the two-sided grill,** place the steak on the grill, close the cover, and cook to the desired degree of doneness, 4 to 5 minutes for medium rare.

◆ **If you are using the grill pan,** cook the steak to the desired degree of doneness, 8 to 10 minutes for medium rare, turning it once midway through the cooking time.

◆ Transfer the steak to a platter and let stand for 5 minutes before serving.

Pork and Lamb

Barbecued Country-Style Ribs

For a down-home meal, add baked beans, coleslaw, and Corn Bread (page 237) to the menu.

SERVES 4

For the sauce

1 tablespoon vegetable oil

1 onion, chopped

2 cloves garlic, minced

$^1/_2$ cup (4 fl oz/125 ml) tomato sauce

$^1/_2$ cup (4 fl oz/125 mg) packed light
or dark brown sugar

$^1/_4$ cup (2 fl oz/60 ml) cider vinegar

1 tablespoon Worcestershire sauce

2 teaspoons Dijon mustard

$^1/_2$ teaspoon salt, plus more as needed

$^1/_2$ teaspoon freshly ground black pepper,
plus more as needed

$^1/_2$ teaspoon hot pepper sauce

$^1/_4$ teaspoon chipotle chile powder or
other pure chile powder

For the ribs

2$^1/_2$ pounds (1.25 kg) country-style pork ribs

Salt and freshly ground black pepper

◆ To make the sauce, in a medium saucepan heat the oil over medium heat. Add the onion and garlic and cook, stirring often, until lightly colored, about 8 minutes. Add the remaining sauce ingredients. Bring the mixture to a simmer and cook, stirring often, until it is very thick and reduced to about ¾ cup, about 15 minutes.

◆ Preheat a large two-sided electric indoor grill or ridged grill pan according to the manufacturer's instructions.

◆ Season both sides of the ribs with salt and pepper.

◆ **If you are using the two-sided grill,** place the ribs on the grill, close the cover, and cook until they are no longer pink next to the bone, about 10 minutes. Check halfway through the cooking time to be sure the ribs are cooking evenly and rearrange them if necessary.

Brush half of the barbecue sauce onto the ribs; turn them with tongs, and brush with the remaining sauce. Continue cooking until the glaze is browned but not burned, 1 to 2 minutes more. Check the ribs often, removing the ones that have browned, and cooking the remaining ribs a little longer.

◆ **If you are using the grill pan,** cook the ribs until they are no longer pink next to the bone, about 18 minutes, turning them once midway through the cooking time. Brush the barbecue sauce onto both sides of the ribs and cook them for a few minutes more until they have browned, turning again.

Pork Tenderloin Medallions with Mustard-Crumb Coating

These tender breaded rounds are delicious topped with applesauce. Pick some up at the store or make your own (microwave two peeled, quartered, and cored cooking apples with 2 tablespoons water and 2 teaspoons sugar until tender, about 7 minutes).

SERVES 4

1¹/₂ cups (3 oz/90 g) fine fresh breadcrumbs (about 3 slices firm white bread)

3¹/₂ tablespoons olive oil

1¹/₂ teaspoons dried thyme leaves, crumbled

1¹/₂ teaspoons minced garlic

¹/₄ teaspoon salt

¹/₄ teaspoon freshly ground black pepper

2 tablespoons regular or coarse-grain Dijon mustard

1 pork tenderloin, about 1 pound (500 g)

✦ In a small bowl, combine the breadcrumbs, $1\frac{1}{2}$ tablespoons of the olive oil, thyme, garlic, salt, and pepper; toss together well. In another small bowl, stir together the mustard and the remaining 2 tablespoons of olive oil.

✦ Cut the tenderloin crosswise into 4 equal sections. At the midpoint of each section, cut nearly but not all the way through; fold open each section like a book to make a larger round. Cover the medallions with plastic wrap and pound with a heavy pan to flatten them to a thickness of about $\frac{1}{2}$ inch (12 mm).

✦ Preheat a two-sided electric indoor grill or ridged grill pan according to the manufacturer's instructions.

✦ Brush both sides of each medallion with some of the mustard mixture, then press the medallion in the breadcrumb mixture.

✦ **If you are using the two-sided grill,** place the medallions on the grill, close the cover, and cook until the pork is no longer pink in the center, about 4 minutes.

✦ **If you are using the grill pan,** cook the medallions until the pork is no longer pink in the center, about 7 minutes, turning them once midway through the cooking time.

✦ Serve immediately

Deluxe Sirloin Burgers
Page 90

**Beef Tenderloin Steaks
with Horseradish Sauce**
Page 112

Thai Beef Salad
Page 92

**Ginger-Marinated
London Broil**
Page 114

Flank Steak Pinwheels
Page 118

Grilled Beef Tacos
Page 96

**Grilled Pork Chops
with Apple-Raisin Chutney**
Page 146

Grilled Sausage & Peppers Alfredo
Page 152

**Pork Tenderloin
with Cider-Molasses Sauce**
Page 150

Middle Eastern
Lamb Skewers
Page 162

Grilled Lamb Sandwiches
with Rosemary-Mustard Sauce
Page 164

Halibut with Sweet-Tart Tomato Sauce
Page 202

**Shrimp Skewers
with Mango Salsa**
Page 174

**Monkfish Medallions
with Salsa Verde**
Page 176

Grilled Vegetable Couscous
Page 208

Asparagus with Orange-Sesame Dressing
Page 206

Grilled Pork Chops
with Apple-Raisin Chutney

These sweet and smoky chops are wonderful served with roasted sweet potatoes and sautéed spinach. The chutney can be made up to two days ahead and reheated just before serving.

SERVES 4

For the chutney

2 teaspoons olive oil

1 small clove garlic, minced

2 Granny Smith apples, unpeeled, cored, and diced

1 cup (8 fl oz/250 ml) orange juice

$^1/_3$ cup (2 oz/60 g) golden raisins

2 teaspoons cider vinegar

$^1/_2$ teaspoon minced canned chipotle chiles

$^1/_4$ teaspoon ground cumin

$^1/_8$ teaspoon salt

Freshly ground black pepper

For the pork

4 bone-in center-cut pork chops, $^1/_2$ inch (12 mm) thick, about $1^1/_2$ pounds (750 g) total

2 teaspoons olive oil

Salt and freshly ground black pepper

photograph on page 135

+ To make the chutney, in a nonstick skillet heat the oil over medium-high heat. Add the garlic and cook, stirring constantly, for 20 seconds. Add the apples and sauté until softened slightly, about 3 minutes.

+ Add the orange juice, raisins, vinegar, chiles, cumin, salt, and pepper. Cook, stirring occasionally, until the mixture has reduced to a sauce consistency, about 8 minutes. Taste and season with additional salt and pepper if needed. Keep the chutney warm.

+ Preheat a two-sided electric indoor grill or ridged grill pan according to the manufacturer's instructions.

+ Rub both sides of the pork chops with the olive oil and season with salt and pepper.

+ **If you are using the two-sided grill,** place the pork chops on the grill, close the cover, and cook until just a trace of pink remains in the center, $2\frac{1}{2}$ to 3 minutes.

+ **If you are using the grill pan,** cook the chops until just a trace of pink remains in the center, 4 to 6 minutes, turning them once midway through the cooking time.

+ Divide the chops among 4 plates and spoon the chutney over the top. Serve immediately.

French Toast Ham & Cheese Sandwiches

If you are making these tasty sandwiches for kids, a firm supermarket-style bread is fine, but adults will probably prefer the firmer texture of a country-style bakery loaf.

SERVES 4

2 large eggs

$^2/_3$ cup (5 fl oz/160 ml) milk

8 thick slices country-style bread, whole wheat, walnut, semolina, or white

4 teaspoons Dijon mustard

4 thick slices smoked ham

4 thick slices cheese, such as Swiss, cheddar, fontina, or muenster

+ In a shallow dish, whisk the eggs until combined and slightly frothy. Add the milk and whisk again to combine.

+ Preheat a large two-sided electric indoor grill or ridged grill pan according to the manufacturer's instructions.

+ Spread 4 slices of the bread with about 1 teaspoon of mustard each. Top each piece of bread with a slice of ham, a slice of cheese, and another slice of bread.

+ Dip both sides of each sandwich briefly in the egg and milk mixture until just saturated.

+ **If you are using the two-sided grill,** place the sandwiches on the grill, close the cover, and cook until the bread is golden and the melted cheese begins to sizzle on the grill, 2 to 4 minutes.

+ **If you are using the grill pan,** cook the sandwiches until the bread is golden and the melted cheese begins to sizzle on the pan, 4 to 8 minutes, turning them once midway through the cooking time.

Variations

Tuna Melt: Replace the mustard and ham filling with 2 cans of tuna mixed with mayonnaise and your favorite seasonings. Divide the tuna among 4 slices of bread. Top with a slice of cheese, if desired, and another slice of bread. Dip the sandwiches in the egg and milk mixture and cook as above.

Breakfast Sandwich: Use cinnamon-raisin bread and a filling of 2 coarsely mashed bananas. Dip the sandwiches in the egg and milk mixture and cook as above. Serve topped with maple syrup.

Pork Tenderloin
with Cider-Molasses Sauce

*Mashed potatoes
and braised bitter
greens are perfect
accompaniments to
the spicy-sweet
flavors of this dish.
Any leftovers will
make great pork
sandwiches.*

SERVES 4

For the sauce

1 teaspoon canola oil

1 large clove garlic, minced

1 jalapeño chile, seeded and minced

1 cup (8 fl oz/250 ml) apple cider

$1/_3$ cup (4 oz/115 g) molasses

$1/_4$ cup (2 fl oz/60 ml) apple cider vinegar

Salt and freshly ground black pepper

For the pork

2 teaspoons chili powder, preferably pure ground

$1^1/_2$ teaspoons coarse salt

2 small pork tenderloins, about $3/_4$ pound (375 g)
each, trimmed of excess fat

photograph on page 137

✦ To make the sauce, in a medium saucepan heat the oil over medium-low heat. Add the garlic and jalapeño and cook, stirring, for about 30 seconds. Stir in the cider, molasses, and vinegar and bring to a boil. Lower the heat and simmer until thickened to a syrup consistency, about 20 minutes. Season with salt and pepper to taste. Cover the sauce and set aside.

✦ Preheat a two-sided electric indoor grill or ridged grill pan according to the manufacturer's instructions.

✦ Combine the chili powder and salt and rub the mixture all over the pork tenderloins.

✦ **If you are using the two-sided grill,** place the tenderloins on the grill, close the cover, and cook until the pork is just slightly pink in the center, about 8 minutes.

✦ **If you are using the grill pan,** cook the pork until it is just slightly pink in the center, about 15 minutes, turning it once midway through the cooking time.

✦ Transfer the pork to a cutting board and let stand for 5 minutes (it will continue cooking and should have just a trace of pink remaining).

✦ Cut the pork crosswise into $1/2$- to $3/4$-inch (12-mm–2-cm) slices. Divide among 4 plates and spoon the sauce over the pork. Serve immediately.

Grilled Sausage & Peppers Alfredo

This dish is tasty but rich with its creamy variation on Alfredo sauce. It comes together quickly and is good for casual entertaining. Although it could be made with hot sausage as well, the heat masks the subtle flavor of fontina. Serve it with a green salad and Italian bread.

SERVES 4

1 large onion, thinly sliced

1 red or yellow bell pepper, cored and thinly sliced

1 tablespoon olive oil

Salt and freshly ground black pepper

1 pound (16 oz/500 g) dried fettuccine or linguine

$^{3}/_{4}$ pound (375 g) sweet Italian sausage (3 links)

$1^{1}/_{4}$ cups (10 fl oz/310 ml) heavy cream

$1^{1}/_{4}$ cups (5 oz/155 g) shredded fontina cheese

2 tablespoons chopped fresh parsley

photograph on page 136

✦ Bring a large pot of water to a boil.

✦ Preheat a two-sided electric indoor grill or ridged grill pan according to the manufacturer's instructions.

✦ In a large bowl, toss the onions and peppers with the oil and season with salt and pepper. Prick the sausages with a fork.

✦ **If you are using the two sided grill,** place the sausages on the grill, close the cover, and cook until browned on all sides (turning if necessary) and the juices run clear, about 4 minutes. Remove the sausages from the grill and cut into ½-inch (12-mm)-thick slices.

Arrange the peppers and onions in a single layer on the grill, and cook until tender, about 3 minutes, stirring occasionally with a wooden spoon.

✦ **If you are using the grill pan,** cook the sausages, onions, and peppers together until the vegetables are tender and the sausages are browned and the juices run clear, about 10 minutes. Turn the vegetables often, and turn the sausages once midway through. Remove from the pan and cut the sausages into ½-inch (12-mm)-thick slices.

✦ Cook the pasta until tender but still slightly chewy, 10 to 12 minutes.

✦ In a medium saucepan, heat the cream over low heat until it starts to simmer. Add the cheese, and stir until smooth. Add the sausages and vegetables and cook until heated through. Remove from the heat. Season with salt and pepper to taste.

✦ When the pasta is cooked, drain it, and transfer to a large shallow serving bowl. Add the sauce and toss to coat. Sprinkle with parsley and serve.

Grilled Pork Chops with Red-Eye Gravy

A modern rendition of a Southern classic. Traditionally the gravy is made just by pouring hot coffee into the skillet after frying ham steaks to deglaze the pan. This version is diluted with chicken broth, but expect a pleasantly bitter edge from the coffee.

SERVES 4

4 bone-in center-cut pork chops, $1/2$ inch (12 mm) thick, about $1^{1}/2$ pounds (750 g) total

1 tablespoon unsalted butter

$1^{1}/2$ cups ($4^{1}/2$ oz/135 g) thinly sliced fresh mushrooms

1 cup (8 fl oz/250 ml) brewed coffee

$3/4$ cup (6 fl oz/180 ml) low-sodium chicken broth

2 teaspoons cornstarch

1 tablespoon bourbon

2 teaspoons olive oil

Salt and freshly ground black pepper

◆ Trim the excess fat and the small tenderloin from each pork chop and cut the trimmings into 1-inch (2.5-cm) pieces. In a 10-inch cast iron skillet, melt half of the butter over medium-high heat. Add the pork trimmings and sear until well browned on all sides, about 5 minutes. Remove the trimmings from the skillet with a slotted spatula and discard.

◆ Add the remaining butter and the mushrooms to the skillet and sauté until they are softened and nicely browned, about 3 minutes. Stir in the coffee and chicken broth. Stir and scrape to deglaze the pan. Bring to a boil, lower the heat, and simmer for 5 minutes.

◆ Meanwhile, in a small dish, stir the cornstarch and bourbon together until smooth. Stir this mixture into the gravy and cook, stirring, until the gravy is thickened slightly, about 2 minutes. Season with salt and pepper to taste. Keep the gravy warm.

◆ Preheat a two-sided electric indoor grill or ridged grill pan according to the manufacturer's instructions.

◆ Rub the pork chops with the olive oil and season with salt and pepper.

◆ **If you are using the two-sided grill,** place the chops on the grill, close the cover, and cook until just a trace of pink remains in the center, about 3 minutes.

◆ **If you are using the grill pan,** cook the chops until just a trace of pink remains in the center, about 6 minutes, turning them once midway through the cooking time.

◆ Divide the chops among 4 plates and spoon the gravy over them. Serve immediately.

Pork Tenderloin
with Pineapple-Chipotle Glaze

The two-sided grill offers a great way to cook pork tenderloin, as demonstrated in this dish with a smoky-sweet glaze. Dried chipotle chiles and canned chipotles in adobo sauce are widely available. Serve with roasted sweet potatoes and black beans with rice.

SERVES 4

For the glaze

$^1/_2$ cup (4 fl oz/125 ml) unsweetened pineapple juice

$^1/_3$ cup (3 fl oz/80 ml) cider vinegar

4 teaspoons unsulphured molasses

$^1/_4$–$^1/_2$ teaspoon minced chipotle chiles, preferably chipotles in adobo sauce

For the pork

2 small pork tenderloins, about $^3/_4$ pound (375 g) each, trimmed of excess fat

Salt and freshly ground black pepper

♦ To make the glaze, in a medium saucepan combine the pineapple juice and vinegar. Bring to a boil and cook, uncovered, over medium heat until reduced to $1/3$ cup (3 fl oz/80 ml), about 10 minutes. Remove from the heat and stir in the molasses and chiles. Set aside. (The glaze can be made up to 2 days ahead and stored, covered, in the refrigerator.)

♦ Preheat a two-sided electric indoor grill or ridged grill pan according to the manufacturer's instructions.

♦ Season the pork with salt and pepper.

♦ **If you are using the two-sided grill,** place the pork on the grill, close the cover, and cook until the pork is seared on all sides, about 4 minutes. Lift the cover and brush the glaze over the pork. Close the cover and cook, turning often, until golden and just slightly pink in the center, 3 to 4 minutes more.

♦ **If you are using the grill pan,** cook until the pork is seared on all sides, about 8 minutes. Brush the glaze over the pork and cook for 6 to 8 minutes more, turning often until golden and just slightly pink in the center.

♦ Transfer the pork to a cutting board and let stand for 5 minutes.

♦ Cut the pork crosswise into $1/2$– to $3/4$-inch thick (12-mm–2-cm) slices. Drizzle any remaining glaze over the meat and serve.

Pita with Grilled Lamb Meatballs & Minted Yogurt Sauce

These hearty pita sandwiches make a great light supper served with a crisp Greek salad of romaine lettuce, feta cheese, and black olives.

SERVES 4

For the sauce

2 cups (1 lb/500 g) plain yogurt

1 clove garlic, minced

2 tablespoons (1 fl oz/30 ml) olive oil

$1^1/_2$ teaspoons red wine vinegar or fresh lemon juice

1 tablespoon chopped fresh parsley

1 tablespoon chopped fresh mint

Salt and freshly ground black pepper

For the meatballs and sandwiches

1 pound (500 g) ground lamb

1 large egg, lightly beaten

1 small yellow onion, grated

1 clove garlic, minced

$1^1/_2$ teaspoons chopped fresh thyme

$1/_2$ teaspoon salt

$1/_4$ teaspoon freshly ground black pepper

4 pita bread rounds, tops sliced off

8 slices tomato

4 slices red onion

◆ To make the sauce, line a strainer with cheesecloth or several moistened paper coffee filters. Set the strainer over a bowl, add the yogurt, cover and refrigerate for 4 to 6 hours or until the yogurt has drained, thickened, and reduced to about 1 cup (8 oz/250 g).

◆ Discard the drained liquid. In a small bowl stir together the thickened yogurt with the garlic, olive oil, vinegar or lemon juice, parsley, and mint. Season the yogurt mixture with salt and pepper to taste. Cover and refrigerate.

◆ To make the meatballs, in a bowl combine the lamb, egg, onion, garlic, thyme, salt, and pepper and mix with your hands until well combined. Shape the meat mixture into sixteen $1\frac{1}{2}$-inch (4-cm) balls.

◆ Preheat a two-sided electric indoor grill or ridged grill pan according to the manufacturer's instructions.

◆ **If you are using the two-sided grill,** place the meatballs on the grill, close the cover, and cook until they are no longer pink in the center, about 3 minutes.

◆ **If you are using the grill pan,** cook until the meatballs are no longer pink in the center, about 5 minutes, turning them several times during cooking to brown them on all sides.

◆ Serve the meatballs in the pita breads with the sliced tomato and onion, and the yogurt sauce.

Lemon-Rosemary Lamb Chops

These savory lamb chops make a nice meal when served with chutney, Couscous with Currants & Pine Nuts (page 232), and roasted carrots.

SERVES 4

2 small cloves garlic, minced

2 tablespoons olive oil

2 teaspoons chopped fresh rosemary

1 teaspoon grated lemon zest

$1/2$ teaspoon salt

$1/2$ teaspoon freshly ground black pepper

8 bone-in lamb loin chops, about $2^1/2$ pounds (1.25 kg) total, trimmed of fat

+ In a small bowl, combine the garlic, olive oil, rosemary, lemon zest, salt, and pepper. Rub this mixture over all the surfaces of the lamb chops and arrange them in a single layer on a platter. Cover the platter with plastic wrap and marinate in the refrigerator for at least 3 hours or overnight.

+ Preheat a two-sided electric indoor grill or ridged grill pan according to the manufacturer's instructions.

+ **If you are using the two-sided grill,** place the lamb chops on the grill, close the cover, and cook, in batches as necessary, until the chops are pink on the inside, 3 to 4 minutes.

+ **If you are using the grill pan,** cook the lamb chops in batches as necessary. Sear the chops until they have grill marks, about 2 minutes per side; then reduce the heat to medium-low and cook, turning occasionally, until pink on the inside, 3 to 5 minutes more.

+ Transfer the lamb chops to a plate and let stand, covered with aluminum foil, for 5 minutes before serving.

Middle Eastern Lamb Skewers

Lamb cut from the leg makes the most tender, succulent skewers. If it's unavailable already boned, ask your supermarket's butcher to bone, trim, and cube the meat for you. If you like, you can serve the skewers with Minted Yogurt Sauce (page 158).

SERVES 4

For the marinade

2 small onions, grated

$^3/_4$ cup (6 fl oz/180 ml) olive oil

1 teaspoon freshly ground black pepper

1 teaspoon dried oregano

1 teaspoon ground cinnamon

1 teaspoon ground cumin

Pinch of cayenne pepper

For the skewers

1 pound (500 g) boneless leg of lamb, trimmed and cut into 1$^1/_2$-inch (4-cm) cubes

1 large red onion, cut into 1-inch pieces

4 plum tomatoes, halved lengthwise and crosswise

2 small green bell peppers, cored and cut into 1$^1/_2$-inch (4-cm) pieces

$^1/_4$ cup olive oil

Salt and freshly ground black pepper

photograph on page 138

✦ To make the marinade, in a shallow, nonreactive dish combine all the marinade ingredients and mix well. Add the lamb cubes and turn them to coat. Cover the dish and refrigerate for 8 to 24 hours.

✦ Preheat a two-sided electric indoor grill or ridged grill pan according to the manufacturer's instructions.

✦ Thread the cubes of lamb alternating with the red onion onto skewers, leaving a little space between the pieces. Discard the used marinade. On separate skewers, thread the tomato pieces alternating with the bell pepper pieces. Brush all of the vegetable skewers with the olive oil and season with salt and pepper.

✦ **If you are using the two-sided grill,** place the vegetable skewers on the grill, close the cover, and cook until the vegetables are tender and browned in spots, about 5 minutes. Transfer them to a platter and keep warm.

Grill the lamb skewers, in batches as necessary, to the desired degree of doneness, 3 to 4 minutes for medium rare.

✦ **If you are using the grill pan,** cook the vegetable skewers until the vegetables are tender and browned in spots, about 10 minutes, turning once midway through the cooking time. Transfer to a platter and keep warm.

Grill the lamb skewers, in batches as necessary, to the desired degree of doneness, 6 to 8 minutes for medium rare, turning once midway through the cooking time.

✦ Transfer the lamb skewers to the same platter as the vegetable skewers, arrange them attractively, and serve immediately.

Grilled Lamb Sandwiches
with Rosemary-Mustard Sauce

Roasted red potatoes and a green salad turn these substantial sandwiches into a meal.

For the lamb

$^{1}/_{4}$ cup (2 fl oz/60 ml) red wine vinegar

2 tablespoons olive oil

4 cloves garlic, chopped

1 teaspoon chopped fresh rosemary

$^{1}/_{4}$ teaspoon freshly ground black pepper

$1^{1}/_{4}$ pounds (625 g) lamb steak, cut from the leg

Salt

For the sauce

$^{1}/_{3}$ cup (3 oz/85 g) mayonnaise (regular or reduced fat)

2 tablespoons plain yogurt

2 teaspoons Dijon mustard

$^{1}/_{2}$ teaspoon chopped fresh rosemary

Freshly ground black pepper

8 slices sourdough bread, $^{1}/_{2}$ inch (12 mm) thick

3 tablespoons olive oil

1 cup (1 oz/30 g) watercress or arugula leaves

✦ To prepare the lamb, in a shallow, nonreactive dish combine the vinegar, olive oil, garlic, rosemary, and pepper. Add the lamb steak and turn it to coat. Cover and refrigerate for 2 to 24 hours.

✦ To make the sauce, in a small bowl whisk together all the sauce ingredients until smooth. Cover and refrigerate for at least 1 hour.

✦ Preheat a two-sided electric indoor grill or ridged grill pan according to the manufacturer's instructions.

✦ Remove the lamb from the marinade, shaking off the excess. Season it with salt on both sides.

✦ **If you are using the two-sided grill,** place the lamb on the grill, close the cover, and cook to the desired degree of doneness, about 4 minutes for medium rare. Transfer the lamb to a cutting board and let it stand for 5 minutes.

✦ **If you are using the grill pan,** cook the lamb to the desired degree of doneness, 8 to 10 minutes for medium rare, turning it once midway through the cooking time. Transfer the lamb to a cutting board and let it stand for 5 minutes.

✦ Brush the bread on both sides with the 3 tablespoons olive oil. Grill until nicely browned, about 1 minute on the two-sided grill or $1\frac{1}{2}$ to 2 minutes per side in the grill pan.

✦ To assemble: Thinly slice the lamb across the grain. Spread some of the sauce onto half of the bread slices. Top those with the lamb, watercress or arugula, and the remaining bread and serve immediately.

photograph on page 139

Seafood

Grilled Tuna Kabobs

The recipe for these pretty and flavorful kabobs especially lends itself to indoor grilling. They make a nice supper when served on a bed of rice pilaf accompanied by sautéed zucchini and summer squash.

SERVES 4

$^1/_4$ cup (2 fl oz/60 ml) olive oil

3 tablespoons fresh lemon juice

$^1/_2$ teaspoon paprika

$1^1/_2$–2 pounds (750 g–1 kg) fresh tuna steaks, cut into 1-inch cubes

24 small whole bay leaves

2 lemons, thinly sliced

2 green, red, or yellow bell peppers, seeded and cut into 1-inch (2.5-cm) squares

16 firm ripe cherry tomatoes

Salt and freshly ground black pepper

Lemon wedges for garnish

+ In a bowl, whisk the oil, lemon juice, and paprika until combined. Add the tuna cubes and stir them to coat. Marinate them at room temperature, stirring occasionally, for 30 minutes or in the refrigerator for 45 minutes.

+ Meanwhile, in a shallow pan, soak the bay leaves in warm water for 30 minutes. Drain and set aside.

+ Preheat a two-sided electric indoor grill or ridged grill pan according to the manufacturer's instructions.

+ Thread skewers with the tuna cubes, bay leaves, lemon, bell pepper, and tomato, leaving a little space between the pieces. Season with salt and pepper to taste.

+ **If you are using the two-sided grill,** place the kabobs on the grill, close the cover, and cook, in batches as necessary, until the tuna is no longer pink in the center, 3 to 4 minutes.

+ **If you are using the grill pan**, cook the kabobs, in batches as necessary, until the tuna is no longer pink in the center, 5 to 6 minutes, turning once midway through the cooking time.

+ Serve the kabobs on a platter garnished with lemon wedges.

Fish Grilled in Grape Leaves

A wrapping of brine-packed grape leaves accentuates the Mediterranean flavors of the marinade and keeps the fish moist during grilling.

SERVES 4

For the marinade

¹/₄ cup (2 fl oz/60 ml) olive oil

2 tablespoons chopped fresh parsley or fennel fronds

2 teaspoons chopped fresh thyme or oregano

Juice of 1 small lemon (about 2 tablespoons)

¹/₂ teaspoon salt

¹/₄ teaspoon freshly ground black pepper

For the fish

4 white fish fillets such as cod, sea bass, hake, pompano, or pollock, about 1–1¹/₂ pounds (500–750 g) total

Bottled grape leaves, rinsed and stems removed

Lemon wedges for garnish

✦ To make the marinade, in a shallow, nonreactive dish whisk together the olive oil, parsley or fennel, thyme or oregano, lemon juice, salt, and pepper. Add the fish fillets, turning them to coat. Cover and refrigerate for 1 to 2 hours.

✦ Preheat a two-sided electric indoor grill or ridged grill pan according to the manufacturer's instructions.

✦ Remove the fish from the marinade, shaking off the excess. Wrap each fillet in 1 or 2 grape leaves, leaving the ends exposed.

✦ **If you are using the two-sided grill,** place the fillets on the grill, close the cover, and cook until they are just opaque in the center, about 4 minutes. (Cook for 2 to 3 minutes per half inch of thickness.)

✦ **If you are using the grill pan**, cook the fillets until they are just opaque in the center, about 7 minutes, turning them once midway through the cooking time. (Cook for 4 to 6 minutes per half inch of thickness.)

✦ Serve the fish with lemon wedges and any juices poured over the top.

Crab Cakes
with Roasted Garlic Aioli

Crab cakes are a hearty New England supper. Serve them with boiled or roasted potatoes and a selection of roasted vegetables. The aioli (garlic mayonnaise) is a great accompaniment and a nice change from tartar sauce.

SERVES 4

For the aioli

2 large heads garlic

1 tablespoon extra-virgin olive oil

1 cup (8 oz/250 g) mayonnaise (regular or reduced fat)

1 tablespoon fresh lemon juice, plus more as needed

Salt and freshly ground black pepper

For the crab cakes

1 large egg, lightly beaten

$^1/_4$ cup (2 oz/60 g) mayonnaise (regular or reduced fat)

$^1/_4$ cup (3 oz/90 g) minced red onion

$^1/_4$ cup ($^3/_8$ oz/10 g) chopped fresh parsley

$^1/_4$ cup (1 oz/30 g) plus $^2/_3$ cup (3 oz/85 g) fine dry breadcrumbs

1 tablespoon coarse-grain mustard

$^1/_2$ teaspoon Worcestershire sauce

$^1/_4$ teaspoon salt

$^1/_4$ teaspoon freshly ground black pepper

1 pound (500 g) fresh lump crabmeat, picked over for bits of shell and cartilage

◆ Preheat the oven to 325°F (165°C).

◆ To make the aioli, remove the papery skin from the garlic. With a sharp knife, cut the top off the garlic, exposing the cloves. Place the garlic on a square of aluminum foil and drizzle with the olive oil. Bring the edges of the foil together and seal. Bake until the cloves are tender, 50 to 60 minutes. When cool enough to handle, slip the cloves out of their skins.

◆ In a blender or food processor, combine the garlic, mayonnaise, and lemon juice; blend until smooth. Season with salt and pepper to taste. The aioli will keep, covered, in the refrigerator for up to 1 week.

◆ To make the crab cakes, in a bowl combine the egg, mayonnaise, onion, parsley, the $1/4$ cup (1 oz/30 g) breadcrumbs, mustard, Worcestershire sauce, salt, and pepper. Stir the mixture until smooth. Add the crabmeat and mix gently. Form into eight $1/2$-inch (12-mm)-thick patties. Spread the remaining $2/3$ cup (3 oz/85 g) breadcrumbs in a shallow dish and dredge the crab cakes until coated on all sides.

◆ Preheat a two-sided electric indoor grill or ridged grill pan according to the manufacturer's instructions.

◆ **If you are using the two-sided grill,** arrange the crab cakes on the grill, close the cover, and cook until they are golden, 4 to 6 minutes.

◆ **If you are using the grill pan,** cook the crab cakes, in batches as necessary, until golden, 6 to 8 minutes, turning carefully midway through the cooking time.

◆ Divide the crab cakes among 4 plates and serve with the aioli.

Shrimp Skewers with Mango Salsa

This easy, fast, and flavorful dish is a great choice for casual weeknight entertaining. A nice substitute for the shrimp would be salmon fillets. Serve the skewers with basmati rice and an avocado-orange salad.

SERVES 4

For the shrimp

1/4 cup (2 fl oz/60 ml) olive oil

3 cloves garlic, thinly sliced

3 tablespoons fresh lime juice

1/2 teaspoon salt

1/4 teaspoon freshly ground black pepper

1–1 1/2 pounds (500–625 g) large shrimp, peeled and deveined

For the salsa

2 ripe mangoes, peeled and diced

4 scallions, white and green parts, trimmed and thinly sliced

1 small jalapeño chile, seeded and very finely diced

2–3 tablespoons chopped fresh cilantro

2 tablespoons fresh lime juice

Lime wedges for garnish

photograph on page 141

✦ To prepare the shrimp, in a small saucepan heat the olive oil and garlic over low heat until fragrant, about 3 minutes. Transfer to a medium bowl.

✦ Add the 3 tablespoons lime juice, salt, and pepper; stir to combine. Cool slightly. Add the shrimp and stir to coat them. Marinate the shrimp at room temperature for 30 minutes, stirring occasionally.

✦ While the shrimp is marinating, make the salsa. In a medium bowl, stir together all the salsa ingredients. Season with salt and set aside.

✦ Preheat a large two-sided electric indoor grill or ridged grill pan according to the manufacturer's instructions.

✦ Thread the shrimp onto skewers, passing the skewer through points near both the head and tail sections of each shrimp, leaving a little space between the pieces.

✦ **If you are using the two-sided grill,** place the skewers on the grill, close the cover, and cook, in batches as necessary, until the shrimp turn pink and are opaque throughout, 2 to 3 minutes.

✦ **If you are using the grill pan,** cook the shrimp, in batches as necessary, until they turn pink and are opaque throughout, 4 to 6 minutes, turning them once midway through the cooking time.

✦ Serve the skewers with lime wedges and the salsa.

Monkfish Medallions with Salsa Verde

If monkfish is unavailable, pair this bright, fresh sauce with any mild white fish—it's also terrific with salmon. Serve the fish with fresh asparagus and rosemary roasted potatoes.

SERVES 4

For the sauce

$^1/_2$ cup ($^1/_2$ oz/15 g) packed parsley leaves

1 tablespoon drained capers

1 clove garlic

$^1/_4$ teaspoon grated lemon zest

1 tablespoon fresh lemon juice

$^1/_4$ cup (2 fl oz/60 ml) extra-virgin olive oil

Salt and freshly ground black pepper

For the monkfish

$1^1/_2$ pounds (750 g) monkfish, trimmed and cut across into 8 medallions about 1 inch (2.5 cm) thick

1 tablespoon olive oil

Salt and freshly ground black pepper

photograph on page 142

◆ To make the sauce, in a food processor combine the parsley, capers, garlic, lemon zest, and lemon juice; pulse until chopped. Add the olive oil and process until pureed, stopping once or twice to scrape down the sides of the bowl. Season the sauce with salt and pepper and set aside.

◆ Preheat a two-sided electric indoor grill or ridged grill pan according to the manufacturer's instructions.

◆ Brush both sides of the monkfish medallions with oil, and season with salt and pepper.

◆ **If you are using the two-sided grill,** place the fish on the grill, close the cover, and cook until the medallions are just cooked through, 1 to 1½ minutes.

◆ **If you are using the grill pan,** cook the fish until the medallions are just cooked through, about 3 minutes, turning them once midway through the cooking time.

◆ Divide the medallions among 4 plates and spoon the sauce over the top of each piece. Serve immediately.

Grilled Sea Scallops on Braised Fennel

In this tasty dish, fennel adds a new dimension to the delicate taste of scallops. If you use a two-sided grill, the liquid from the scallops that collects in the drip tray makes a delicious sauce when spooned over the cooked scallops.

SERVES 4

For the fennel

2 bulbs fennel
2 tablespoons unsalted butter
$^1/_2$ cup (4 fl oz/125 ml) water
Salt and freshly ground black pepper
$^1/_4$ cup (1 oz/30 g) freshly grated Parmesan cheese

For the marinade and scallops

2 tablespoons olive oil
2 tablespoon fresh lemon juice
$^1/_2$ teaspoon salt
$^1/_4$ teaspoon freshly ground black pepper
$1^1/_2$ pounds (750 g) dry sea scallops

+ To prepare the fennel, cut away the feathery tops from the fennel bulbs and trim the bottoms. Finely chop $1/4$ cup ($1/3$ oz/10 g) of the feathery fronds and set aside. Cut the fennel bulbs in half lengthwise and then cut lengthwise again into $1/4$-inch (6-mm)-thick slices, leaving some of the core on each slice to hold it together.

+ In a 4-quart Dutch oven, melt the butter over medium heat. Add the fennel and stir until it starts to brown, 5 to 7 minutes. Add the water and season with salt and pepper. Bring to a simmer; reduce the heat to low, cover, and simmer, stirring occasionally, until the fennel is very tender, about 20 minutes. Remove from the heat and stir in the cheese and 3 tablespoons of the reserved fennel fronds. Season with salt and pepper and keep warm.

+ To prepare the scallops, in a small bowl mix the olive oil, lemon juice, salt, pepper, and the remaining 1 tablespoon chopped fennel fronds; whisk to combine. Add the scallops and toss them to coat. Marinate the scallops at room temperature, stirring occasionally, for 20 to 30 minutes. Thread the marinated scallops onto skewers, leaving a little space between the pieces.

+ Preheat a two-sided electric indoor grill or ridged grill pan according to the manufacturer's instructions.

+ **If you are using the two-sided grill,** place the skewers on the grill, close the cover, and cook, in batches as necessary, until the scallops are golden on the outside and opaque in the center, 3 to 4 minutes.

+ **If you are using the grill pan,** cook the scallops, in batches as necessary, until they are golden on the outside and opaque in the center, 6 to 8 minutes, turning them once midway through the cooking time.

+ To serve, spoon the fennel on 4 warmed plates and place the scallop skewers on top.

Tuna Burgers
with Wasabi Mayonnaise

Serve this decidedly different burger with a tomato and red onion salad tossed with cilantro. The wasabi root is the Japanese version of horseradish. Wasabi powder can be found in the Asian foods section of most supermarkets.

SERVES 4

For the mayonnaise

2 teaspoons wasabi powder

2 teaspoons water

$1/2$ cup (4 oz/125 g) mayonnaise (regular or reduced fat)

For the burgers

1 pound (500 g) fresh tuna

4 scallions, finely chopped

1 large clove garlic, minced

4 teaspoons minced fresh ginger

4 teaspoons soy sauce

2 teaspoons Dijon mustard

2 teaspoons mayonnaise (regular or reduced fat)

4 teaspoons olive oil

4 hamburger buns

◆ To make the mayonnaise, in a small bowl stir together the wasabi powder and water. Stir in the mayonnaise. Let the mixture stand for at least 20 minutes.

◆ Using a chef's knife, chop the tuna until it resembles ground beef (this will take a few minutes; do not use a food processor). In a bowl, combine the tuna, scallions, garlic, ginger, soy sauce, mustard, and mayonnaise. Form the mixture into four 1-inch (2.5-cm)-thick hamburger-shaped patties.

◆ Preheat a two-sided electric indoor grill or ridged grill pan according to the manufacturer's instructions.

◆ Brush the tuna burgers on both sides with the olive oil.

◆ **If you are using the two-sided grill,** place the tuna burgers on the grill, close the cover, and cook until they are nicely browned on the outside and still slightly pink in the center, 1 to 1½ minutes.

◆ **If you are using the grill pan,** cook the tuna burgers until they are nicely browned on the outside and still slightly pink in the center, 2 to 4 minutes, turning them once midway through the cooking time.

◆ While the tuna burgers are cooking, toast the buns.

◆ Spread the toasted hamburger buns generously with the wasabi mayonnaise, place a tuna burger on each one, and serve immediately.

Salmon Fillets
with Maple-Balsamic Glaze

*Simple but
sophisticated, a
drizzle of tart
vinegar syrup
makes the
succulent salmon
even sweeter. Serve
the salmon with
steamed white rice
and a sauté of
julienned carrots
and summer
squash.*

SERVES 4

For the glaze

^{1}/$_2$ cup (4 fl oz/120 ml) balsamic vinegar
^{1}/$_4$ cup (2 fl oz/60 ml) maple syrup
3 tablespoons rice wine vinegar
^{1}/$_2$ teaspoon salt
^{1}/$_4$ teaspoon freshly ground black pepper

For the salmon

1 center-cut skinless salmon fillet, about 1^1/$_2$ pounds
    (750 g) total, cut into 4 pieces
Salt and freshly ground black pepper

◆ To make the glaze, in a small saucepan combine all the glaze ingredients. Bring the mixture to a boil over high heat and cook, stirring, until it is syrupy and reduced to about $\frac{1}{2}$ cup (4 fl oz/120 ml), about 6 minutes. Set the glaze aside.

◆ Preheat a two-sided electric indoor grill or ridged grill pan according to the manufacturer's instructions.

◆ To prepare the salmon, remove any bones from the fillets and season both sides with salt and pepper.

◆ **If you are using the two-sided grill,** place the fish on the grill, close the cover, and cook until the fillets are golden on the outside and just opaque in the center, about 3 minutes. (Cook for 2 to 3 minutes per half inch of thickness.)

◆ **If you are using the grill pan,** cook the fish until the fillets are golden on the outside and just opaque in the center, about 6 minutes, turning them once midway through the cooking time. (Cook for 4 to 6 minutes per half inch of thickness.)

◆ Serve each fillet drizzled with the glaze.

Sea Bass in Thai Coconut Sauce

If sea bass is hard to find, halibut or grouper would be an excellent substitute. Basmati rice and sautéed baby bok choy or steamed broccoli are ideal accompaniments for the rich, fragrant sauce.

SERVES 4

For the sauce

1¹/₂ tablespoons canola oil

2 large shallots, finely chopped

3 cloves garlic, finely chopped

1 stalk fresh lemongrass, trimmed and coarsely chopped

1 tablespoon green curry paste

2 teaspoons grated lime zest

2 (14 oz/430 ml) cans unsweetened coconut milk

2 tablespoons fresh lime juice

2 tablespoons coarsely chopped fresh cilantro

For the fish

1¹/₂ pounds (750 g) sea bass fillet, cut into 4 pieces

Salt and freshly ground black pepper

✦ To make the sauce, in a large saucepan heat the oil over medium heat. Add the shallots and garlic and cook, stirring constantly, for 1 minute. Add the lemongrass and stir for 1 minute more. Add the curry paste and lime zest and gradually stir in the coconut milk. Bring the sauce to a boil, lower the heat, and simmer it slowly until very fragrant and thickened slightly, about 15 minutes. Set the sauce aside to cool completely.

✦ Place the fish in a shallow, nonreactive dish just large enough to hold the pieces in a single layer. Pour about half of the coconut sauce over the fish pieces and turn them to coat well. Cover the dish and refrigerate for 1 hour. Strain the remaining sauce into a clean saucepan.

✦ Preheat a two-sided electric indoor grill or ridged grill pan according to the manufacturer's instructions.

✦ Heat the saucepan of strained sauce over low heat. Remove the fish from the marinade, wiping off the excess. Season all sides of the fish with salt and pepper.

✦ **If you are using the two-sided grill,** arrange the fish on the grill, close the cover, and cook until the fish is just cooked through, 2 to 3 minutes. (Cook for 2 to 3 minutes per half inch of thickness.)

✦ **If you are using the grill pan,** cook the fish until it is just cooked through, 4 to 6 minutes, turning once midway through the cooking time. (Cook for 4 to 6 minutes per half inch of thickness.)

✦ Remove the sauce from the heat, stir in the lime juice and cilantro, and season with salt to taste. Divide the fish among 4 plates and spoon the sauce over the top. Serve immediately.

Grilled Bluefish & Potatoes

The rich flavor of a darker-fleshed fish like bluefish marries well with the garlic and rosemary of this dish from the Adriatic, but you can also use any firm white fish.

SERVES 4

1–1^1/$_2$ pounds (500–750 g) bluefish fillets, cut into 4 pieces

Salt and freshly ground black pepper

5 tablespoons (3 fl oz/80 ml) olive oil, divided

1^1/$_2$ tablespoons fresh lemon juice

2 teaspoons chopped fresh rosemary

1 pound (500 g) boiling potatoes, unpeeled and cut into ^{1}/$_4$-inch (6-mm)-thick slices

1^1/$_2$ teaspoons chopped fresh garlic

^{1}/$_2$ teaspoon salt

- ◆ Season both sides of the fish fillets with salt and pepper.

- ◆ In a shallow, nonreactive dish, combine 3 tablespoons of the olive oil with the lemon juice and rosemary. Add the fish fillets and turn them a few times to coat. Cover the dish and refrigerate for 1 hour.

- ◆ Preheat a large two-sided electric indoor grill according to the manufacturer's instructions.

- ◆ In a bowl, combine the potatoes, garlic, salt, and the remaining 2 tablespoons of olive oil.

- ◆ Spread the potato slices evenly over the grill, close the cover, and cook for 6 minutes. Open the grill and turn the potatoes over with tongs. Continue cooking until the potatoes are tender, about 6 minutes more. Open the grill and place the fish fillets, skin side down, on top of the potatoes, pouring any juices from the dish over them. Cook until the fish is opaque in the center, 3 to 5 minutes. (Cook for 2 to 3 minutes per half inch of thickness.)

- ◆ Divide the fish and potatoes among 4 plates and serve immediately.

Grilled Fish Tacos

The fish for this San Diego specialty is often deep-fried, but grilling it indoors is lighter, faster, and easier. Serve these soft tacos with lots of napkins, because they are as messy as they are fun to eat.

SERVES 4

For the sauce

$1/3$ cup (3 oz/80 g) mayonnaise (regular or reduced fat)

$1/3$ cup (3 fl oz/80 ml) sour cream or yogurt

$1/4$ cup (1 oz/30 g) chopped red onion

$1/4$ cup ($1/3$ oz/10 g) chopped fresh cilantro

For the tacos

1 tablespoon olive oil

1 teaspoon hot chili powder

$1/4$ teaspoon salt

8 large or 12 small corn tortillas

1 pound (500 g) white fish fillets, such as pollock, red snapper, haddock, halibut, mahi mahi or cod

For serving

2 cups (6 oz/180 g) shredded green cabbage

1 cup (8 fl oz/250 ml) Quick Tomato Salsa (page 25) or store bought

2 avocados, pitted, peeled, and sliced

2 limes, cut into wedges

◆ To make the sauce, in a small bowl whisk together the mayonnaise, sour cream or yogurt, onion, and cilantro.

◆ In a medium bowl, whisk together the olive oil, chili powder, and salt; set aside.

◆ Preheat oven to 300°F (150°C). Preheat a large two-sided electric indoor grill or large grill pan according to the manufacturer's instructions.

◆ Directly on top of electric or gas stove burners, lightly toast both sides of the tortillas; wrap them in foil and set in the oven to keep warm.

◆ Cut the fish fillets crosswise into 1-inch (2.5-cm)-wide strips. Add the fish to the reserved olive oil mixture and toss until evenly coated.

◆ **If you are using the two-sided grill,** arrange the fish pieces in an even layer on the grill, close the cover, and cook until the fish is just opaque in the center, about 2 minutes, depending on the variety of fish. Transfer the fish to a platter.

◆ **If you are using the grill pan,** arrange the fish pieces in an even layer and cook until just opaque in the center, about 4 minutes, depending on the variety of fish. Turn once midway through the cooking time. Transfer the fish to a platter.

◆ To assemble, put a few tablespoons of cabbage in the middle of a tortilla, top with some of the fish, a spoonful of the sauce, a spoonful of salsa, some avocado slices, and a squeeze of lime juice. Fold up and eat.

Prosciutto-Wrapped Shrimp Skewers

These Mediterranean-inspired skewers make a wonderful, light dinner when served with bruschetta and a big spinach salad tossed with roasted red peppers and feta cheese.

SERVES 4

For the marinade

2 tablespoons fruity Italian white wine

2 tablespoons olive oil

1 tablespoon fresh lemon juice

Eight 2-inch (5-cm) strips lemon zest

3 large cloves garlic, minced

1 teaspoon fresh thyme leaves or $^1/_2$ teaspoon dried

$^1/_2$ teaspoon crumbled bay leaf

Freshly ground black pepper

For the skewers

16 jumbo shrimp (about 1 pound/500 g), peeled and deveined

2 medium zucchini, trimmed and cut lengthwise into $^1/_8$-inch (3-mm)-thick slices

8 slices prosciutto, cut paper thin, trimmed of excess fat, and cut in half lengthwise

◆ To make the marinade, in a shallow, nonreactive dish combine all the marinade ingredients and mix well. Add the shrimp and turn them to coat. Cover the dish and refrigerate it for 30 minutes to 2 hours.

◆ Preheat a two-sided electric indoor grill or ridged grill pan according to the manufacturer's instructions.

◆ **If you are using the two-sided grill,** arrange the zucchini slices on the grill, close the cover, and cook until just soft and pliable, about 3 minutes. Let them cool slightly.

To prepare the skewers, remove the shrimp from the marinade, reserving the lemon strips. Wrap 1 slice of prosciutto around a shrimp, then wrap it with a zucchini slice. Thread the shrimp onto a skewer. Repeat with the remaining shrimp, prosciutto, and zucchini, putting 4 shrimp on each skewer, leaving a little space between the pieces. Thread 2 of the reserved lemon strips on each skewer.

Place the skewers on the grill, close the cover, and cook until the shrimp is just cooked through, about 3 minutes.

◆ **If you are using the grill pan,** cook the zucchini slices, in batches as necessary, until just soft and pliable, about 5 minutes, turning once midway through the cooking time. Let them cool slightly.

Prepare the skewers as described above. Cook until the shrimp is just cooked through, about 6 minutes, turning once midway through the cooking time.

◆ Arrange the skewers on a platter, garnish with thyme sprigs, and serve immediately.

Sesame Salmon Steaks

A golden crust of sesame seeds enhances the delicate taste of salmon. A great way to serve this dish is on a bed of Asian Slaw (page 226). Add rice or Asian noodles to complete the meal.

SERVES 4

^{1}/$_3$ cup (1 oz/30 g) sesame seeds

1 teaspoon salt

4 salmon steaks, about 1 inch (2.5 cm) thick, center bones removed

✦ In a small saucepan or skillet toast the sesame seeds over low heat, stirring constantly, until golden and fragrant, about 4 minutes. Stir in the salt, then transfer them to a plate to cool.

✦ Preheat a two-sided electric indoor grill or ridged grill pan according to the manufacturer's instructions.

✦ Dip both sides of each salmon steak in the sesame seed mixture to coat.

✦ **If you are using the two-sided grill,** place the fish on the grill, close the cover, and cook until the salmon is barely opaque in the center, 4 to 5 minutes.

✦ **If you are using the grill pan,** cook the salmon until it is barely opaque in the center, 8 to 10 minutes, turning once midway through.

✦ Transfer the salmon to a serving dish.

photograph opposite

Sesame Salmon Steaks
with Asian Slaw
Pages 192 and 226

Spinach Calzone
Page 216

**Bruschetta with Tomatoes,
Beans & Fresh Herbs**
Page 238

**Polenta Panini
with Artichokes,
Olives & Feta**
Page 222

Black Bean Quesadillas
Page 218

Grilled Peach Melba
Page 248

Grilled Pears with Balsamic Vinegar
& Goat Cheese
Page 244

Grilled Pineapple Sundae
Page 242

Halibut with Sweet-Tart Tomato Sauce

*This is a good dish
to serve when
entertaining,
because the sauce
can be made a day
or two ahead. If you
like, you could
substitute sea
scallops, shrimp, or
cod for the halibut.*

SERVES 4

For the sauce

1 tablespoon canola oil

1 onion, finely chopped

3 cloves garlic, minced

1 (14 oz/440 g) can tomatoes, drained and chopped

$^1/_2$ cup ($2^1/_2$ oz/75 g) green olives, pitted and sliced

$^1/_4$ cup ($1^1/_2$ oz/45 g) dried currants or raisins

$^1/_3$ cup (3 fl oz/80 ml) water

1 teaspoon chopped fresh oregano, or $^1/_4$ teaspoon
 dried

Salt and freshly ground black pepper

2 tablespoons chopped fresh cilantro or parsley

1 tablespoon fresh lime or lemon juice

For the fish

$1^1/_2$ pounds (750 g) halibut steak, cut into 4 pieces

Canola oil

Salt and freshly ground black pepper

Lime or lemon wedges for garnish

photograph on page 140

✦ To make the sauce, in a large skillet heat the oil over medium heat. Add the onion and cook, stirring, until softened, about 5 minutes. Add the garlic and stir until fragrant, about 1 minute more. Add the tomatoes, olives, currants or raisins, water, and oregano. Reduce the heat to low, cover the skillet and simmer, stirring occasionally, until the tomatoes have melted into a sauce, about 10 minutes. Season with salt and pepper. (The sauce will keep, covered, in the refrigerator for 2 days. Reheat it before continuing.) Season the sauce with the cilantro or parsley and lime or lemon juice. Keep the sauce warm.

✦ Preheat a two-sided electric indoor grill or ridged grill pan according to the manufacturer's instructions.

✦ Brush the halibut pieces with oil and season with salt and pepper.

✦ **If you are using the two-sided grill,** place the fish on the grill, close the cover, and cook until it is browned and crisp on top and opaque in the center, 4 to 7 minutes. (Cook for 2 to 3 minutes per half inch of thickness.)

✦ **If you are using the grill pan,** cook the fish until it is browned and crisp on top and opaque in the center, 8 to 10 minutes. (Cook for 4 to 6 minutes per half inch of thickness.) Turn the fish once midway through the cooking time.

✦ Transfer the fish to warmed plates and spoon the warm sauce over the top.

Vegetables and Vegetarian Entrees

Asparagus
with Orange-Sesame Dressing

Peeling the fibrous outer skin from asparagus stalks is worth the trouble— the asparagus will cook more evenly, be more tender, and have a brighter color.

SERVES 4

For the dressing

2 teaspoons sesame seeds
$^1/_4$ cup (2 fl oz/60 ml) orange juice
$^1/_4$ teaspoon sugar
1 teaspoon olive oil
1 teaspoon dark sesame oil
$^1/_4$ teaspoon grated orange zest

For the asparagus

1 pound (500 g) fresh asparagus
2 teaspoons extra-virgin olive oil
$^1/_2$ teaspoon salt
$^1/_4$ teaspoon freshly ground black pepper

photograph on page 144

✦ To make the dressing, in a small saucepan stir the sesame seeds constantly over medium heat until deeply golden and fragrant, about 4 minutes; transfer them to a small saucer to cool.

✦ Add the orange juice and sugar to the pan; increase the heat to high and cook, swirling the pan, until the juice has thickened and reduced to 1 tablespoon, about 3 minutes. Whisk in the olive and sesame oils, orange zest, and sesame seeds. Set aside.

✦ To prepare the asparagus, snap off the woody bottom of each spear at the point near the base where the stalk begins to bend. With a vegetable peeler, remove the skin from the stalk by scraping from just below the tip toward the base.

✦ In a shallow dish, gently toss the peeled asparagus with the olive oil, salt, and pepper.

✦ Preheat a large two-sided electric indoor grill or ridged grill pan according to the manufacturer's instructions.

✦ **If you are using the two-sided grill,** arrange the asparagus in a single layer, close the cover, and cook just until tender, about 8 minutes.

✦ **If you are using the grill pan,** cook the asparagus just until tender, about 10 minutes, turning it several times.

✦ Serve the asparagus hot or at room temperature, drizzled with the dressing.

Grilled Vegetable Couscous

*This couscous
makes a terrific
vegetarian main
course, particularly
when served with
Romesco Sauce
(page 26). It's also
good paired with
Middle Eastern
Chicken Kabobs
(page 66) or simply
grilled lamb chops.*

SERVES 4

1 fennel bulb, trimmed and thinly sliced

1 large red bell pepper, cored and quartered

1 small zucchini, trimmed and cut lengthwise
    into $1/4$-inch (6-mm)-thick slices

1 small yellow squash, trimmed and cut lengthwise
    into $1/4$-inch (6-mm)-thick slices

3 portobello mushrooms

$1/4$ cup (2 fl oz/60 ml) plus 3 tablespoons olive oil

1 teaspoon salt, plus more as needed

Freshly ground black pepper

1 cup (3 oz/80 g) uncooked instant couscous

1 teaspoon grated lemon zest

1 tablespoon fresh lemon juice

2 scallions, thinly sliced

$1/4$ cup ($3/8$ oz/10 g) chopped fresh parsley

photograph on page 143

◆ Preheat a two-sided electric indoor grill or ridged grill pan according to the manufacturer's instructions.

◆ In a large, shallow baking dish or roasting pan place the vegetables (keeping the types of vegetables as separate as possible). Toss them with the $\frac{1}{4}$ cup (2 fl oz/60 ml) of olive oil and season with salt and pepper to taste.

◆ **If you are using the two-sided grill,** place the vegetables on the grill in a single layer, close the cover, and cook, in batches as necessary, until browned and tender, 3 to 5 minutes (depending on the vegetable; the squashes take less time than the fennel and peppers). Transfer to a cutting board.

◆ **If you are using the grill pan,** cook the vegetables, in batches as necessary, until browned and tender, 6 to 10 minutes (depending on the vegetable; the squashes take less time than the fennel and peppers). Turn the vegetables midway through the cooking time. Transfer to a cutting board.

◆ Meanwhile, cook the couscous according to the package directions; keep it covered.

◆ Cut the vegetables into 1- to $1\frac{1}{2}$-inch (2.5–4 cm) pieces. Transfer the couscous to a large bowl and fluff with a fork. Toss the couscous with the remaining 3 tablespoons of the olive oil, the salt, pepper, lemon zest, and lemon juice. Toss in the cut-up vegetables, the scallions, and parsley.

◆ Serve warm or at room temperature.

Grilled Eggplant
with Miso-Ginger Dressing

To turn this casual side dish into a fabulous first course, cut the grilled eggplant slices into strips, arrange over a bed of bitter greens, and sprinkle with toasted sesame seeds. Miso can be found in the Asian foods section of the grocery store or at Asian markets.

SERVES 4

For the dressing

1/4 cup (2 fl oz/60 ml) orange juice

2 1/2 tablespoons white miso

2 teaspoons grated fresh ginger

1 clove garlic, minced

1 teaspoon toasted sesame oil

1/2 teaspoon Asian chile oil

1/4 cup (2 fl oz/60 ml) rice wine vinegar

1/3 cup (3 fl oz/80 ml) canola oil

For the eggplant

1 medium eggplant, cut crosswise into 1/2-inch (12-mm)-thick slices

2 tablespoons coarsely chopped fresh basil

✦ To make the dressing, in a bowl combine the orange juice, miso, ginger, garlic, sesame oil, and chile oil and whisk until smooth. Whisk in the vinegar. Whisking constantly, slowly drizzle in the canola oil.

✦ In a shallow, nonreactive dish, arrange the eggplant slices. Pour half of the dressing over the eggplant and turn the slices to coat them well. Cover the dish and let it stand at room temperature for 30 minutes to 2 hours. Set aside the remaining dressing.

✦ Preheat a two-sided electric indoor grill according to the manufacturer's instructions.

✦ Remove the eggplant slices from the marinade, shaking off the excess. Arrange the slices on the grill, close the cover, and cook until the eggplant is browned and tender, 7 to 8 minutes.

✦ Divide the eggplant among 4 plates and drizzle with the reserved dressing. Sprinkle with fresh basil and serve immediately.

Cheddar-Potato Cakes

Crisp and cheesy, these potato cakes make a great side dish for grilled steak. Add a seeded and minced jalapeño if you want some heat, or make small potato cakes and top them with tomato salsa for an easy hors d'oeuvre.

1 large egg

1 teaspoon ground cumin

$^1/_4$ teaspoon salt

$^3/_4$ pound (12 oz/375 g) Yukon Gold or other thin-skinned potatoes

$1^1/_2$ cups (6 oz/185 g) shredded sharp cheddar cheese

$^1/_4$ cup ($^3/_4$ oz/30 g) chopped chives or scallions

+ In a bowl, whisk together the egg, cumin, and salt until slightly frothy.

+ Peel and coarsely grate the potatoes. Working over another small bowl, firmly squeeze the potatoes a handful at a time to extract as much liquid as possible. Add the squeezed potatoes to the beaten egg.

+ Add the cheese and chives or scallions to the potato mixture and stir them together thoroughly.

+ Preheat a two-sided electric indoor grill according to the manufacturer's instructions.

+ Spoon the potato mixture onto the grill in 8 generous mounds, in batches as necessary, and close the cover. Cook for 4 minutes, then turn over, and cook until the potatoes are tender all the way to the center and golden on both sides, about 4 minutes more.

Southwestern Pumpkin Patties

These golden spiced patties are slightly soft, like refried beans. Serve them with rice simmered with peas for a hearty vegetarian supper the whole family will love.

SERVES 4

1 tablespoon olive oil, plus more for brushing

^{3}/$_4$ cup (3 oz/90 g) chopped onion

2 teaspoons hot chili powder

1 teaspoon ground cumin

1 teaspoon minced garlic

1 (15 oz/470 g) can black beans, rinsed and drained

^{3}/$_4$ cup (6 oz/185 g) canned unseasoned pumpkin puree

^{1}/$_2$ cup (1^1/$_2$ oz/45 g) finely crushed tortilla chips

2 tablespoons chopped fresh cilantro

^{1}/$_2$ teaspoon salt

Sour cream and tomato salsa for garnish

◆ In a medium skillet, heat the 1 tablespoon of olive oil over medium heat. Add the onion and cook, stirring, until softened, about 5 minutes. Add the chili powder, cumin, and garlic and cook until fragrant, about 2 minutes more. Transfer to a bowl.

◆ Add the beans, pumpkin, tortilla chips, cilantro, and salt to the onion mixture; stir together well and let stand for 2 minutes.

◆ Preheat a two-sided electric indoor grill or ridged grill pan according to the manufacturer's instructions.

◆ Shape the mixture into 4 patties and brush both sides with olive oil.

◆ **If you are using the two-sided grill,** place the patties on the grill, close the cover, and cook until they are browned and heated through, about 3 minutes.

◆ **If you are using the grill pan,** cook the patties until they are browned and heated through, about 6 minutes, turning once midway through the cooking time.

◆ Serve topped with sour cream and salsa.

Spinach Calzone

Like pizza, calzones inspire creativity. Try other fillings such as cooked sausage, chicken, or ham, sun-dried tomatoes, or fresh herbs. Avoid overly moist fillings like tomato sauce, which can make the crust soggy. You can make your own pizza dough, but it's easier to buy it already prepared at the supermarket.

SERVES 4

$^3/_4$ cup (6 oz/190 g) ricotta cheese

$^1/_2$ cup (2 oz/60 g) freshly grated Parmesan cheese

$^1/_4$ teaspoon salt, plus more as needed

1 tablespoon olive oil

2 whole cloves garlic

4 cups (4 oz/120 g) fresh spinach leaves, washed, thoroughly dried, and stemmed

Freshly ground black pepper

1 pound (500 g) prepared pizza dough

$^1/_4$ cup chopped bottled roasted red peppers, blotted dry

1 cup (4 oz/125 g) shredded mozzarella cheese

photograph on page 194

✦ If the ricotta seems watery, let it drain in a sieve for about 10 minutes. In a small bowl, stir together the ricotta, Parmesan cheese, and salt; set aside.

✦ In a skillet, heat the oil over medium heat. Add the garlic and stir, turning, until it is colored on all sides, about 3 minutes. Pour into a small bowl and set aside. Add the spinach to the skillet and stir until completely wilted, about 2 minutes. Transfer the spinach to a plate and season with salt and pepper to taste.

✦ On a floured work surface, roll out the pizza dough into a 14-inch (35-cm) circle; if the dough seems springy, let it relax for several minutes. Spread the ricotta mixture over one half of the dough circle, leaving a 1-inch (2.5-cm) border uncovered. Top the ricotta with the spinach, sprinkle with the red peppers, then sprinkle with the mozzarella cheese.

✦ Moisten the uncovered border of the dough with water and fold the top half of the dough over the filling. Press the edges together firmly, then fold them over again and press with the tines of a fork. Make two small cuts in the top of the crust with scissors or sharp knife to allow steam to escape. Brush the top of the calzone with the reserved garlic oil, discarding the cloves.

✦ Preheat a large two-sided electric indoor grill according to the manufacturer's instructions.

✦ Gently lift the calzone onto the grill, close the cover, and cook until the crust is nicely browned and the calzone is cooked all the way through, about 8 minutes.

✦ Slide the calzone onto a cutting board or cookie sheet and let it stand for several minutes. Cut the calzone into wedges and serve.

Black Bean Quesadillas

*Good for lunch,
dinner, or as part
of a Southwestern-
style brunch,
Mexico's version of
the grilled cheese
sandwich is easy to
embellish. Serve
with a jicama and
orange salad and
Mexican beer.*

SERVES 4

For the quesadillas

1 (15 oz/470 g) can black beans, rinsed

1 jalapeño chile, seeded and minced

2 cups (8 oz/250 g) shredded Monterey Jack or
cheddar cheese

1 cup (7 oz/220 g) diced fresh tomatoes

$1/2$ cup ($1^1/2$ oz/45 g) thinly sliced scallion greens

$1/4$ cup ($3/8$ oz/10 g) chopped fresh cilantro

2 teaspoons ground cumin

1 teaspoon ground coriander

$1/2$ teaspoon dried oregano

Salt and freshly ground black pepper

8 flour tortillas

For garnish

Sour cream

Prepared tomato salsa

Lime wedges

photograph on page 197

✦ In a large bowl, mix the black beans, jalapeño, cheese, tomatoes, scallion, cilantro, cumin, coriander, oregano, salt, and pepper. Toss gently to combine.

✦ Place a flour tortilla on a flat surface. Spread $1/8$ of the bean and cheese mixture on the lower half of the tortilla, leaving a $1/2$-inch (12-mm) border. Fold the tortilla in half (the tortilla will form a half-moon shape) and set aside. Repeat with the remaining tortillas and filling. The quesadillas will keep, covered, in the refrigerator for up to 2 hours.

✦ Preheat a large two-sided electric indoor grill or ridged grill pan according to the manufacturer's instructions.

✦ **If you are using the two-sided grill,** place two quesadillas on the grill, close the cover, and cook until the quesadillas are golden and the filling is heated through, about 3 minutes. Set the quesadillas aside on a warm platter and keep them warm. Repeat with the remaining quesadillas.

✦ **If you are using the grill pan,** place two quesadillas on the pan and cook until they are golden and the filling is heated through, about 6 minutes, turning very carefully midway through the cooking time. Set the quesadillas aside on a warm platter and keep them warm. Repeat with the remaining quesadillas.

✦ To serve, cut the quesadillas into wedges and garnish with sour cream, salsa, and lime wedges.

Grilled Tofu
with Tomato-Olive Salad

For a lively change of pace from the usual Asian seasonings, this tofu takes on the flavors of the Mediterranean. Don't be tempted to skip pressing and draining the tofu or the dish will be soggy. Serve with toasted pita bread.

SERVES 4

For the tofu

1 (15 oz/470 g) package extra-firm tofu, drained

$^1/_2$ cup (4 fl oz/125 ml) fresh lemon juice

$^1/_3$ cup (3 fl oz/80 ml) olive oil

3 large cloves garlic, minced

1 teaspoon dried rosemary, crumbled

1 teaspoon salt

Freshly ground black pepper

For the salad

1 ripe tomato, diced

$^1/_2$ cup ($2^1/_2$ oz/80 g) coarsely chopped imported black olives

1 clove garlic, minced

1 teaspoon grated lemon zest

1 tablespoon olive oil

$^3/_4$ cup ($1^1/_2$ oz/45 g) coarsely chopped watercress or arugula

Salt and freshly ground black pepper

◆ To prepare the tofu, line a baking sheet with plastic wrap. Cut the tofu in half crosswise, then cut each piece in half horizontally and place on the baking sheet. Cover the tofu with another sheet of plastic wrap. Top this with another baking sheet, then weight the top sheet with a heavy object. Refrigerate for 45 minutes to press out the excess moisture from the tofu.

◆ In a glass pie plate, combine the lemon juice, olive oil, garlic, rosemary, and salt and pepper to taste. Uncover the baking sheets and pour off the liquid from the tofu. Place the tofu in the marinade and turn the pieces to coat. Cover the pie plate and marinate the tofu for 1 to 2 hours, turning it once.

◆ Preheat a two-sided electric indoor grill or ridged grill pan according to the manufacturer's instructions.

◆ To make the salad, in a bowl combine the tomato, olives, garlic, lemon zest, and oil and set aside.

◆ Remove the tofu from the marinade, shaking off the excess.

◆ **If you are using the two-sided grill,** arrange the tofu on the grill, close the cover, and cook until it is nicely browned, $2^1/_2$ to 3 minutes.

◆ **If you are using the grill pan**, cook the tofu until it is nicely browned, about 6 minutes, turning it once midway through the cooking time.

◆ Divide the tofu among 4 plates. Toss the watercress or arugula with the tomato mixture and season with salt and pepper to taste. Spoon the salad over the tofu and serve immediately.

Polenta Panini
with Artichokes, Olives & Feta

Serve these golden grilled Italian "sandwiches" (panini) with sliced vine-ripened tomatoes as a light supper or serve them on their own as an appetizer. Polenta is available precooked in cylindrical tubes in well-stocked markets and Italian delis.

<small>SERVES 4</small>

1 (18 oz/560 g) tube prepared plain polenta, chilled for easier slicing

1 (14 oz/440 g) can artichoke hearts

$^1/_2$ cup ($2^1/_2$ oz/60 g) pitted and chopped black olives such as Kalamata

$^3/_4$ cup ($3^3/_4$ oz/120 g) crumbled feta cheese

$^1/_4$ cup (1 oz/30 g) Italian-style dry breadcrumbs

2 tablespoons olive oil

photograph on page 196

+ Cut the polenta crosswise into about sixteen $\frac{1}{4}$-inch (16-mm)-thick slices.

+ Drain the artichoke hearts; hold each one, right side up, under cool running water to rinse away the brine, then invert and firmly squeeze each one to remove all the moisture. Cut them lengthwise into thin slices.

+ Preheat a large two-sided electric indoor grill or ridged grill pan according to the manufacturer's instructions.

+ On 8 of the polenta slices, arrange a layer of sliced artichoke hearts. Sprinkle with some of the olives, then with some of the feta cheese. Press the remaining polenta slices on top.

+ Place the breadcrumbs in a shallow dish. Brush both sides of each polenta sandwich with oil, then press it into the breadcrumbs to coat all sides.

+ **If you are using the two-sided grill,** place the panini on the grill, close the cover, and cook until they are golden, about 3 minutes.

+ **If you are using the grill pan,** cook the panini until they are golden, about 6 minutes, turning over very carefully midway through the cooking time.

+ Divide the panini among 4 plates and serve.

Side Dishes and Accompaniments

Asian Slaw

This variation on coleslaw features the refreshing tastes of mint and cilantro and a light oil and vinegar dressing. It goes especially well with Sesame Salmon Steaks (page 192).

SERVES 4

1/2 cup (2 oz/60 g) very thinly sliced red onion

2 tablespoons rice wine vinegar

1 tablespoon vegetable oil

1 teaspoon sugar

1/2 teaspoon salt

3 cups (9 oz/270 g) finely shredded Napa or Chinese cabbage

2 medium carrots, grated

2 tablespoons chopped fresh mint

2 tablespoons chopped fresh cilantro

✦ In a large bowl, cover the onion with cold water; set it aside to soak for at least 10 minutes.

✦ Drain the water from the onion; add the vinegar, oil, sugar, and salt and toss together. Add the cabbage, carrot, mint, and cilantro and toss again.

✦ Serve chilled or at room temperature.

photograph on page 193

Tomato, Mozzarella & Basil Salad

Few ingredients go together better than ripe summer tomatoes, fresh mozzarella, and fragrant basil. Try to find the tiny balls of mozzarella called bocconcini.

SERVES 4 TO 6

$^3/_4$ pound (375 g) fresh mozzarella cheese, drained

4 tablespoons (2 fl oz/60 ml) extra-virgin olive oil

Salt and freshly ground black pepper

12 fresh basil leaves, thinly sliced

2 tablespoons coarsely chopped fresh parsley

2 pints (12 oz/375 g) round or pear-shaped cherry tomatoes

$^1/_4$ cup ($1^1/_2$ oz/45 g) oil-cured olives such as Kalamata

✦ If using large balls of mozzarella, cut into $^1/_2$-inch (12-mm) dice. If using the smaller size, cut into quarters. In a bowl, toss the cheese with 2 table-spoons of the oil and salt and pepper to taste. Add half the basil and half the parsley; toss gently.

✦ If using round cherry tomatoes, cut them in half; if using the pear-shaped tomatoes, leave them whole. In a bowl, combine the tomatoes with the remaining 2 tablespoons of oil, salt, and pepper to taste, and the remaining basil and parsley; toss gently.

✦ Mound some of the mozzarella mixture onto the center of each plate. Make a ring of tomatoes around the edge of the cheese and garnish with the olives.

Three-Bean, Three-Pepper Salad

Two Mexican pantry staples—beans and peppers—are featured here, with three different varieties of each playing the central roles. Start testing the beans for doneness early, as cooking times vary greatly with age and variety. If you want a really quick salad, you could substitute drained canned beans.

SERVES 4 TO 6

1/2 cup (3 1/2 oz/105 g) dried black beans

1/2 cup (3 1/2 oz/105 g) dried pinto beans

1/2 cup (3 1/2 oz/105 g) dried red or kidney beans

1 yellow bell pepper

1 red bell pepper

1 fresh poblano chile pepper

1/4 cup (2 fl oz/60 ml) red wine vinegar

1 teaspoon salt

1/2 teaspoon freshly ground black pepper

1 canned chipotle chile in vinegar or adobo sauce, stemmed, seeded, and minced (optional)

2/3 cup (5 fl oz/160 ml) olive oil

1 red onion, finely diced

✦ Sort through all the beans, keeping them separate, and discard any misshapen beans or stones. Rinse well. Place each bean variety in a separate saucepan and add enough water to cover generously. Bring each saucepan to a boil, reduce the heat to medium low, cover, and simmer until the smallest bean is cooked through and creamy inside, about $1\frac{1}{2}$ hours.

✦ Drain all the beans in a colander (they can be mixed at this time) and spread them out on a plate to cool slightly.

✦ Meanwhile, remove the stems, seeds and ribs from the bell peppers and the poblano chile. Cut the peppers into a $\frac{1}{4}$-inch (6-mm) dice, or a size as close as possible to that of the cooked beans.

✦ In a large bowl, whisk together the vinegar, salt, black pepper and chipotle chile, if using. Slowly add the oil, whisking constantly. Toss in the peppers, onion, and warm beans and mix well.

✦ Cover and refrigerate for at least 2 hours or as long as overnight. Serve chilled.

Sesame-Green Bean Salad

Wasabi powder is very hot, so use less the first time you make this dish if you are not familiar with its spicy flavor.

SERVES 4

1 pound (500 g) green beans

1 teaspoon wasabi powder

2 teaspoons water

2 tablespoons rice vinegar

1 clove garlic, minced

1 teaspoon sesame oil

1 teaspoon soy sauce

1 tablespoon sesame seeds, toasted

✦ Bring a pan of salted water to a boil. Add the beans and cook for 3 minutes. Plunge the beans into cold water, drain, and set them aside to cool.

✦ In a jar with a screw top, combine the wasabi powder and water. Shake until they are blended and let stand for 5 minutes. Add the vinegar, garlic, sesame oil, soy sauce, and sesame seeds and shake vigorously to blend.

✦ In a bowl, toss the beans with the dressing and serve.

Saffron Rice

Here's a great recipe for your basic repertoire. It goes well with many chicken and fish dishes that call for a mildly flavored but still intriguing accompaniment.

SERVES 4

2 tablespoons dry white wine

Pinch of saffron threads, crumbled

1 tablespoon olive oil

1 small onion, finely chopped

$^1/_2$ teaspoon salt

1 cup (7 oz/220 g) basmati rice

2–2$^1/_4$ cups (16–20 fl oz/500–560 ml) water

✦ In a small bowl, combine the wine and the saffron threads. Set aside in a warm place.

✦ In a saucepan, heat the oil over medium heat. Add the onion and salt; cook, stirring, until softened, about 5 minutes. Add the rice and the saffron mixture; stir to coat. Add the water and bring to a simmer. Reduce the heat to low; cover and simmer until the rice is tender and the water has been absorbed, about 15 minutes. Remove the saucepan from the heat. Let stand, covered, for 5 minutes, then fluff and serve.

Couscous with Currants & Pine Nuts

This simple side dish makes a great accompaniment to many of the recipes in this book, especially the Lemon-Rosemary Lamb Chops (page 160).

SERVES 4

1 (14 oz/440 g) can chicken broth
$^1/_4$ cup (2 fl oz/60 ml) water
1 clove garlic, minced
$^1/_2$ cup (2$^1/_2$ oz/80 g) diced red bell pepper
$^1/_4$ teaspoon salt
Pinch of saffron threads
2 cups (6 oz/160 g) instant couscous
$^1/_2$ cup (1$^1/_2$ oz/45 g) finely sliced scallion greens
$^1/_4$ cup (1 oz/40 g) toasted pine nuts
$^1/_4$ cup (1$^1/_2$ oz/45 g) dried currants
$^1/_4$ cup (2 fl oz/60 ml) olive oil
2 tablespoons chopped fresh mint
Salt and freshly ground black pepper

✦ In a saucepan, combine the chicken broth, water, garlic, bell pepper, salt, and saffron. Bring to a boil and remove from the heat. Immediately add the couscous and stir. Cover and set aside until all the liquid is absorbed, about 8 minutes. Fluff couscous with a fork and stir in the scallions, pine nuts, currants, oil, and mint. Stir to combine. Season with salt and pepper to taste.

✦ Serve warm or at room temperature.

Ribbon Pasta Salad

A creamy pasta salad makes a good accompaniment to simple grilled chicken or beef dishes.

SERVES 4 TO 6

For the salad

8 ounces (250 g) dried tagliatelle pasta
8 ounces (250 g) Belgian endive, finely shredded
1 head (3$^1/_2$ oz/100 g) radicchio, finely shredded
4 ounces (125 g) Gruyère cheese shavings
$^1/_2$ large red bell pepper, thinly sliced

For the dressing

2 tablespoons lemon juice
$^1/_4$ cup (2 fl oz/60 ml) olive oil
2 tablespoons light cream
1 tablespoon mayonnaise (regular or reduced fat)
2 tablespoons snipped fresh chives
Salt and freshly ground black pepper

✦ In a large pot of boiling salted water cook the pasta until al dente. Run the pasta under cold water and drain. Set it aside to cool. In a large bowl, combine the remaining salad ingredients with the pasta.

✦ In a small bowl whisk together all the dressing ingredients. Pour the dressing over the salad and toss well. Serve at room temperature.

Old-Fashioned Potato Salad

A regular feature on American tables since the 19th century, potato salad is a natural accompaniment to grilled meats and sandwiches. Use tiny new potatoes if you can find them. Otherwise any small red potato will work fine.

SERVES 6

For the salad

1 teaspoon salt

2^{1}/$_{2}$ pounds (1.25 kg) small red potatoes, unpeeled

3 ribs celery, cut into ^{1}/$_{4}$-inch (6-mm)-thick slices

^{1}/$_{4}$ cup (1^{1}/$_{2}$ oz/45 g) finely diced red onion

1 tablespoon finely chopped fresh parsley for garnish

For the dressing

^{1}/$_{2}$ cup (4 oz/125 g) sour cream

^{1}/$_{2}$ cup (4 oz/125 g) mayonnaise (regular or reduced fat)

1 tablespoon mustard seeds

1 scallion, including the tender green top, finely chopped

^{1}/$_{4}$ cup (^{1}/$_{3}$ oz/10 g) finely chopped fresh parsley

1 teaspoon dry mustard

^{1}/$_{4}$ teaspoon salt

^{1}/$_{8}$ teaspoon freshly ground black pepper

✦ Bring a large saucepan three-quarters full of water to a boil. Add the salt and then the potatoes. Boil until the potatoes are tender but slightly resistant when pierced with a fork, 15 to 25 minutes depending on the size of the potatoes. Drain and, when cool enough to handle, cut the unpeeled potatoes into 1-inch (2.5-cm) pieces.

✦ In a large bowl, combine the potatoes, celery, and onion and toss briefly to mix. Set aside.

✦ To make the dressing, in a small bowl stir together all the dressing ingredients, mixing well.

✦ Pour the dressing over the potato mixture. Using a large spoon, mix well, being careful not to break up the potatoes. For the best flavor, cover and chill at least 2 hours before serving. Sprinkle the tablespoon of parsley over the top and serve.

Spicy Peanut Noodles

These Asian-inspired noodles are especially good with Grilled Sesame Chicken (page 38). Like all pasta recipes, timing the cooking of the noodles with the rest of the meal is the trick, so it really helps to have all your ingredients prepped before you begin.

SERVES 4

10 ounces (315 g) dried linguine

$1/2$ cup (4 fl oz/125 ml) Satay Sauce (page 78)

$1/2$ cup (4 fl oz/125 ml) hot water

1 cup (3 oz/90 g) thinly sliced scallions, dark and light green parts

1 teaspoon toasted sesame seeds (optional)

◆ Cook the linguine in boiling salted water until al dente, 8 to 10 minutes.

◆ In a large bowl, whisk the Satay Sauce, water, and scallions until smooth. (The sauce will be quite thin; the pasta will quickly absorb it.) Set aside.

◆ Drain the pasta and add it to the reserved sauce; toss to coat.

◆ Sprinkle the pasta with the sesame seeds, if using them, and serve.

Corn Bread

The quickest of quick breads, corn bread pairs particularly well with grilled pork dishes.

SERVES 6

1 cup (5 oz/155 g) yellow cornmeal
1 cup (5 oz/155 g) all-purpose flour
1 teaspoon salt
1 tablespoon baking powder
1 cup (8 fl oz/250 ml) milk
2 tablespoons honey
2 eggs, well beaten
$^1/_3$ cup (3 oz/90 g) unsalted butter, melted and cooled
$^1/_2$ cup (3 oz/90 g) corn kernels, fresh or frozen, (thawed)

✦ Preheat the oven to 400° F (200° C). Grease an 8-inch (20-cm) square baking pan with butter.

✦ In a large bowl, mix together the cornmeal, flour, salt, and baking powder. In a large measuring cup, whisk together the milk, honey, and eggs.

✦ Using a wooden spoon, stir the egg mixture into the cornmeal mixture, mixing well. Stir in the melted butter and then gently mix in the corn kernels. Pour the batter into the prepared baking pan.

✦ Bake the corn bread until the center is firm to the touch, 18 to 20 minutes. Cut it into squares and serve hot.

Bruschetta with Tomatoes, Beans & Fresh Herbs

Bruschetta is a garlic-scented toast brushed with good-quality olive oil. You can use a variety of toppings: marinated roasted peppers, cured meats, or in this case tomatoes, beans, and fresh herbs.

SERVES 4

For the topping

1 cup (6 oz/185 g) seeded and diced ripe tomato

$3/4$ cup ($5^1/2$ oz/170 g) cannellini beans, freshly cooked, or canned, well-drained

$1/4$ cup ($1^1/4$ oz/37g) seeded and diced cucumber

2 tablespoons thinly sliced green onion

1 tablespoon fresh oregano leaves, or $1^1/2$ teaspoons dried

1 tablespoon chopped fresh basil or $1^1/2$ teaspoons dried

3 tablespoons balsamic vinegar

2 tablespoons extra-virgin olive oil

Salt and freshly ground black pepper

For the bruschetta

8 slices baguette or Italian bread, $2^1/2$ inches (6 cm) wide and $1/2$ inch (12 mm) thick

1 large clove garlic, cut in half

4 teaspoons olive oil

photograph on page 195

+ To make the topping, in a bowl combine all the topping ingredients, and season with salt and pepper to taste. Toss well, cover the bowl, and refrigerate for at least 1 to 2 hours or for up to 2 days to allow the flavors to blend.

+ Preheat a two-sided electric indoor grill or ridged grill pan according to the manufacturer's instructions.

+ **If you are using the two-sided grill,** brush one side of the bread slices with olive oil, and place them on the grill. Close the cover and cook until they have grill marks, $1\frac{1}{2}$ to 2 minutes.

+ **If you are using the grill pan,** brush one side of the bread with the olive oil, and cook until they have grill marks, about 2 to 3 minutes, turning midway through the cooking time.

+ Rub a cut side of the garlic over the side of the bread brushed with olive oil. Mound the topping on the garlic and olive oil side of each bread slice. Transfer to a platter and serve immediately.

Desserts

Grilled Pineapple Sundae

You may find this tropical dessert reminds you of a piña colada. It is worth looking for coconut ice cream. but if you can't find it. vanilla works very well. If possible try to find a "supersweet" pineapple.

SERVES 4

^{1}/2 cup (3^1/2 oz/105 g) packed light brown sugar

2 tablespoons dark rum

2 tablespoons water

2 tablespoons fresh lime juice

1 tablespoon canola oil

^{1}/2 pineapple, peeled, cored, and cut into ^{1}/2-inch (12-mm)-thick slices

4 scoops coconut or vanilla ice cream

Toasted coconut for garnish

photograph on page 200

+ In a small saucepan, combine the brown sugar, rum, and water. Bring to a simmer over medium heat and cook until the mixture thickens slightly, 3 to 5 minutes. Remove the saucepan from the heat and stir in 1 tablespoon of the lime juice. Keep the sauce warm.

+ In a bowl, combine the oil and the remaining 1 tablespoon of lime juice. Add the pineapple slices and toss them to coat.

+ Preheat a two-sided electric indoor grill or ridged grill pan according to the manufacturer's instructions.

+ **If you are using the two-sided grill,** arrange the pineapple slices in a single layer on the grill and close the cover. Cook until the pineapple is seared on all sides, about 4 minutes.

+ **If you are using the grill pan,** arrange the pineapple slices in a single layer. Cook until the pineapple is seared on all sides about 8 minutes, turning once midway through the cooking time.

+ Transfer the pineapple slices to a cutting board and cut them into chunks. Transfer the chunks to the saucepan with the reserved sauce and stir them to coat.

+ Serve the warm pineapple chunks over scoops of coconut ice cream and garnish with toasted coconut.

Grilled Pears with Balsamic Vinegar & Goat Cheese

A lovely, simple dessert to end a Mediterranean-inspired meal, this is a great way to reintroduce the cheese course. Look for the best balsamic vinegar and goat cheese available in your area. Serve the pears with a nice dessert wine.

SERVES 4

4 ripe pears, such as Bosc or Bartlett

1 tablespoon vegetable oil

1 tablespoon fresh lemon juice

4 ounces (125 g) aged goat cheese, cut into 4 pieces

4 teaspoons good quality balsamic vinegar

photograph on page 199

✦ Trim the stems and bottoms off of the pears and peel. With a melon baller, scoop the cores from the bottom of the pears. Cut each pear lengthwise into 8 slices about ¾ inch (2 cm) thick. In a large bowl, combine the oil and lemon juice. Add the pear slices and toss them to coat.

✦ Preheat a two-sided electric indoor grill or ridged grill pan according to the manufacturer's instructions.

✦ **If you are using the two-sided grill,** arrange half the pears in a single layer on the grill, close the cover, and cook until the pears are seared on both sides and heated through, 3 to 4 minutes. (Due to the curved nature of the fruit, it may be necessary to turn the fruit midway through the cooking time to get grill marks.) Remove the pears from the grill and keep them warm. Repeat with the remaining pears.

✦ **If you are using the grill pan,** arrange half the pears in a single layer in the pan and cook until they are seared and heated through, 6 to 8 minutes, turning them once midway through the cooking time. Remove the pears from the grill and keep them warm. Repeat with the remaining pears.

✦ Arrange the pears and the goat cheese on 4 dessert plates. Drizzle each serving with 1 teaspoon balsamic vinegar and serve.

Cranberry-Stuffed Apple Slices with Maple Syrup

Make these tender apples for a quick weeknight dessert or as part of a weekend breakfast. The crispy breadcrumb topping will remind you of traditional Brown Betty.

$^1/_2$ cup (2 oz/60 g) dried cranberries

1 slice firm white bread

1 tablespoon butter, melted

$^1/_8$ teaspoon ground cinnamon

3 large cooking apples such as Golden Delicious or Rome

$^1/_2$ cup (4 fl oz/125 ml) maple syrup, warmed

◆ In a small bowl cover the cranberries with water and a small plate or plastic wrap. Microwave on high power for 1 minute; set the bowl aside. (Alternatively, you can soften the cranberries in a small saucepan by simmering them with water for 1 minute.)

◆ In a food processor, pulse the bread to make breadcrumbs; you need ½ cup (1 oz/30 g). Transfer to a small bowl and toss well with the butter and cinnamon.

◆ Peel and core the apples and cut them crosswise into about eight ½-inch (12-mm)-thick slices. (Or peel and slice them, then remove the cores with a small round cutter or paring knife.)

◆ Preheat a large two-sided electric indoor grill according to the manufacturer's instructions.

◆ Drain the cranberries and put some in the center of each apple slice, pressing them into an even layer. Sprinkle each apple with some of the breadcrumb mixture.

◆ Place the apples on the grill, close the cover, and cook until the apples are tender when poked with a wooden skewer, about 3 minutes. Serve immediately, topped with the warm maple syrup.

Grilled Peach Melba

A new take on the dessert created in honor of Dame Nellie Melba, a 19th-century Australian opera singer. For a variation, the peaches and sauce could be served on slices of toasted pound cake.

SERVES 4

For the sauce

1 (12 oz/375 g) package unsweetened individually quick-frozen raspberries

$^1/_2$ cup (4 oz/125 g) sugar

$^1/_4$ cup (2 fl oz/60 ml) water

2 tablespoons Chambord or other raspberry-flavored liqueur

1 teaspoon cornstarch

For the peaches

1 tablespoon vegetable oil

1 tablespoon fresh lemon juice

4 ripe peaches, peeled, pitted, and cut lengthwise into $^1/_2$-inch (12-mm)-thick slices

4 scoops vanilla ice cream

photograph on page 198

✦ In a medium saucepan, combine the raspberries, sugar, and water. Cook over medium-low heat, stirring occasionally, until the raspberries have broken down into a sauce, about 5 minutes. Transfer the sauce to a fine sieve set over a bowl and strain, pressing on the solids, until only seeds remain. Return the sauce to a clean saucepan and bring to a simmer over low heat.

✦ In a small bowl, combine the raspberry-flavored liqueur and cornstarch; slowly whisk the cornstarch mixture into the simmering raspberry sauce. Cook, stirring constantly, until the sauce is slightly thickened. Transfer the sauce to a bowl. (The sauce will keep, covered, in the refrigerator, for up to 1 week. Warm the sauce before serving.)

✦ Preheat a two-sided electric indoor grill or ridged grill pan according to the manufacturer's instructions.

✦ In a large bowl, combine the oil and lemon juice. Add the peaches and toss them to coat.

✦ **If you are using the two-sided grill,** arrange half the peaches in a single layer, close the cover, and cook until they are seared on both sides and heated through, 3 to 4 minutes. (Due to the curved nature of the fruit, it may be necessary to turn the fruit midway through the cooking time to get grill marks.) Remove the peaches from the grill and keep them warm. Repeat with the remaining peaches.

✦ **If you are using the grill pan,** arrange half the peaches in a single layer and cook until they are seared and heated through, 6 to 8 minutes, turning them once midway through. Remove from the grill and keep warm. Repeat with the remaining peaches.

✦ To serve, place a scoop of ice cream in 4 bowls and top with the warm peaches and raspberry sauce.

Butter-Rum Grilled Bananas

A decadent little treat, eaten right out of the skin, and as easy as an island breeze. Substitute orange juice for the rum, if you prefer.

S<small>ERVES</small> 4

4 medium bananas, unpeeled
4 tablespoons (2 oz/60 g) butter
$^1/_4$ cup (2 oz/60 g) packed light brown sugar
1 tablespoon dark rum

✦ Preheat a two-sided electric indoor grill or ridged grill pan.

✦ **If you are using the two-sided grill,** place the bananas on the grill, close the cover, and cook until the skins are blackened and the flesh is soft, but not collapsed, about 10 minutes.

✦ **If you are using the grill pan,** cook the bananas until the skins are blackened and the flesh is soft, but not collapsed, about 15 minutes, turning them once.

✦ Meanwhile, in a small saucepan, stir the butter and brown sugar together over medium-high heat until combined and bubbling thickly. Remove from the heat and stir in the rum.

✦ Transfer the bananas to 4 plates and cut a lengthwise slit in the skin, following the natural curve. Pull back the skin and make diagonal slashes in the flesh. Drizzle the sauce over the tops of the bananas and serve.

Index

Italic numbers refer to photographs.

Credits

Recipe on page 227 from *Pizzeria* by Evan Kleiman; recipe on page 228 from *Cantina* by Mary Sue Milliken and Susan Feniger; recipe on page 233 by Jane Hann in *The Barbecue Cookbook;* recipes on pages 234 and 237 from *Diner* by Diane Rossen Worthington; recipe on page 238 from *Trattoria* by Mary Beth Clark.